MW00952223

Einherjar

Gnostic Warriors of the North

~

Way of the Einherjar, Vol. I

Einherjar

Gnostic Warriors of the North

Way of the Einherjar
Vol. I

Roland Jos. L'Heureux

HAR'S HALL

PUBLISHING, U.S.A.
2017

Einherjar—Gnostic Warriors of the North:
Way of the Einherjar, Vol. 1

Folkgard of Holda & Odin / Har's Hall Publishing,
subsidiary divisions of
Runekenhof, Temple of the Northern Mystery Tradition, Inc., ULC
a non-profit religious corporation
Apache Junction, USA.
2017

Copyright © 2017 by Roland Jos. L'Heureux

All rights reserved. Except for brief passages quoted by reviewers, no part of this publication may be reproduced or transmitted in any form or by any means, electronic or mechanical, including photocopying, recording, or by any information storage and retrieval system, without permission in writing from the author.

ISBN-13:978-1519779397
ISBN-10:1519779399

Edited by Debra C. L'Heureux and Roland Jos. L'Heureux
Interior design, graphics, typeset, and production
by Roland Jos. L'Heureux

Inside Cover Image: The Valknútr—*Knot of the Slain.* Recognized as the mystical symbol of the Einherjar, Odin's shamanic warriors, the Valknútr, or Valknut, is typically worn by those who have consecrated themselves as "living dead" to Odin.

To contact the author, write:
roland.northerngnostic@gmail.com
or
Rev. Roland Jos. L'Heureux, DM.
Runekenhof, Temple of the Northern Mystery Tradition, Inc., ULC
P.O. Box 2658
Apache Junction, AZ., 85117-2658

DEDICATED
to
THE ODINIC MYSTERIES

Hung I was on the windswept tree;
Nine full nights I hung,
Pierced by a spear, a pledge to the god,
To Odin, ***myself to myself,***
On that tree, which none can know the source
From whence its root has run.

None gave me bread, none brought a horn.
Then low to earth I looked.
I caught up the runes, roaring I took them,
And fainting, back I fell.

Nine mighty lays I learned from the son
Of Bolthorn, Bestla's father,
And a draught I had of the holy mead
Poured out of Ordrerir.

Then fruitful I grew, and greatly to thrive,
In wisdom began to wax.
A single word to a second word led,
A single poem a second found.

–Odin's Song,
Hávamál, stanzas 138 – 141
(emphasis added)

Your ancestors called it magic,

you call it science,

I come from a place

where they are one and the same.[1]

TABLE OF CONTENTS

AUTHOR'S NOTES

References to religious, sacred, or spiritual text throughout this work demonstrate the existence of a relationship between that text cited and the thought, idea, principle, or concept being discussed and does not necessarily imply or attribute any specific authority to that text. Any authoritative weight attributed to religious, sacred, or spiritual text cited throughout this work is left to each individual reader's conscience.

Use of capital letters for third-person personal pronouns (i.e. He/She) when referencing deities stems from a contemporary, 21st century element of respect and veneration, as well as an aid in textural criticisms, and not from any Victorian superstition.

In any general instance of the use God(s), or any similar non-specific epitaph, the author always intends to imply duel gendered, multiple beings. The term "God," for instance, should be understood as "God(s)/Goddess(es)" unless otherwise indicated by the author in the text.

Though a member of various and several exoteric and esoteric organizations at the time of this publication, and though my sentiments and ideas herein might certainly be shared by those who walk a similar spiritual path as my own, I do not speak for or on behalf of any entity but my own self. I speak from the empirical truths upon which I base my life and life's decisions, truths which stem from my own Asatru studies and experiences; supported here, naturally, within a scholastic framework and template.

End notes and the bibliography adhere to the Chicago Manual of Style (16th ed.) and are provided for academic integrity, as source material for further study, and to demonstrate the references' common (i.e., public) distribution in honor of oaths taken and here upheld.

~ Sub Rosa

Einherjar—Gnostic Warriors of the North

ABBREVIATIONS

a.k.a. —— also known as

BCE —— before the common era

c. —— Lat. *circa*, about, around

CE —— common era

ed. —— editor, edition

etc. —— Latin, *et cetera*, and the rest

Fra. —— Latin, *Frater*, brother

Gk. —— Greek

Lat. —— Latin

Einherjar—Gnostic Warriors of the North

LIST OF CHARTS AND TABLES

Einherjar—Gnostic Warriors of the North

LIST OF DIAGRAMS AND IMAGES

Einherjar—Gnostic Warriors of the North

ACKNOWLEDGMENTS

Hail to my Family, Friends, and Folk who were inspirational, encouraging, and supportive during the production of this book, especially:

my lovely wife and gythja, Debra;
our clan matriarch, Carol;
our son, Sean; our daughter Maret and son-in-law Trevin;
our grand-daughter, Kori; and,
our kindred sister, Teresa,

my sincerest thanks to you all.

Einherjar—Gnostic Warriors of the North

PREFACE

Before our gods and chosen warriors do I pledge, by my solemn word, that I shall always uphold—with honor, dignity and courage—the lifelong commitment to Odin's Einherjar, our folk, and our gods. This I will do on my word and unwavering commitment.
Through body, spirit and soul.

It was just after celebrating my forty-forth birthday that I discovered Ron McVan's book, *Temple of Wotan: Holy Book of the Aryan Tribes.*[2]

My previous mainstream Christian upbringing and adult experience included initiation and training in Roman Catholicism, Eastern Orthodoxy, Protestantism, Christian Science, and The Church of Jesus Christ of Latter-day Saints (Mormon).

I began my studies in and of the occult sciences in late 1999. Initially I studied Christian Gnosticism under mentors like Stephan A. Hoeller, Manly P. Hall, and Roy Masters while associating myself with the Rosicrucian Fellowship (Max Heindel), the Anthroposophical Society (Rudolph Steiner), and the Church of Light (C. C. Zain).

Over time I gained experience with initiatory instruction and training via my affiliation with The Hermetic Order of the Golden Dawn; Fraternitus Lux Occulta; Builders of the Adytum, Temple of the Holy Qabalah and Sacred Tarot; and, the Ancient and Mystical Order Rosæ Crucis, AMORC (the latter of which I am a current affiliate as a member and continuous student).

It was not until reading Ron's book though that I noticed all these pieces of the puzzle begin to fall into place, seeing things from above the labyrinth as it were. Within the Norse Mysteries and the ancient folk religion of Asatru I discovered that *royal road* to my Self—a terrain perfectly cleared to accommodate my individual psyche and naturally suited to my very DNA makeup. Unlike my previous religious experiences,[3] Asatru appealed to my conscience; satisfied my logical thought processes; challenged my individual level of intelligence; and provided endless opportunity to pursue my interest in and application of esoteric psychology and gnostic philosophy.[4]

As for my Norse studies over the years, in addition to typical intellectual investigation in Norse mythology, lore, history, runology, etc., I also assimilated and consolidated the teachings of Stephen McNallen, Valgard Murray, Edred Thorsson (a.k.a. Dr. Stephen Flowers), and Bil Linzie with that of Ron McVan's, creating a personal theosophy through which I am able to experience my own individual spiritual journey from within the established and collective worldview of Asatru.[5]

During the last thirteen years since making my blood-oath however, I have heart achingly witnessed Asatruar fail to nourish and maintain or truly establish this type of symbiotic relationship with the Mysteries and Magic of our religion, either because of a lack of solid external instruction and guidance or a lack of internal and conscious awareness regarding Asatru's living myths and its life changing spiritual path.

Adding to the current literary resources aimed at assisting modern seekers and practitioners in the understanding and application of Asatru, *Einherjar—Gnostic Warriors of the North: Way of the Einherjar, Vol. 1,* presents an anthology of kindred discussions and practical application exercises which have been found profitable for applying, living, and managing one's Asatru journey and spiritual growth along the way.

In this current work, I begin by examining the validity, mission, and esoteric system of training outlined in Norse mythology for Odin's ancient secret society of shamanic knights—the Einherjar.

Systematically, we start by examining several basic and essential aspects of ancient psychological and metaphysical thought as a review of fundamental gnostic philosophy. From there we develop a historical and theoretical backdrop for the Einherjar mythos itself. We then consider literary symbols within Norse mythology which reveal not only an ancient Norse initiatory system of instruction, but its intended use and obligation as well. Finally, demonstrating its functionality and practical application even today, this perennial wisdom is presented as an aid for readers in the raising of their own levels of consciousness and the development of a more virtuous and noble character.

With horn held high then…for the Folk! HAIL!

Roland Jos. L'Heureux
Thorrablot, 2017

INTRODUCTION
From Whence Have You Come?

...the fate of humanity in the near future will bring man together much more than has hitherto been the case—to fulfill a common mission for humanity. But the individuals belonging to the several peoples will only be able to bring their free, concreate contributions to this joint mission if they have, first of all, an understanding of the folk to which they belong.

—Rudolf Steiner[6]

One of my first mentors—a Jesuit priest, Martinist initiate, and Christian mystic in his own right, Frater I:.N:. I shall call him—insisted that I study, of all things, my own ancestral "old testament". Fra. I:.N:. often stressed that, while adopted by the Christian church to act as the "catholic," or "universal," folk religion for all its initiates, the Old Testament of the Bible is actually specific to the tribes of Israel, as it is a record of *their* ancient religion and how *they* interpreted the divine within *their* particular culture.[7]

Being of South American descent himself, Fra. I:.N:., in conjunction with and compliment of his own studies in the

1

Christian Mysteries, had made it a point to also study the ancient religions of the Incan, Aztec, and Mayan tribes.[8] It was Fra. I:.N:.'s connection with, appreciation for, and perspective from his ancestral religion which he considered the most significant contributing factors in his own spiritual pilgrimage and religious experience.

As the "Northern-gnostic" among his protégés, Fra. I:.N:. naturally directed my studies toward the Pre-Christian folk religion of the indigenous Europeans (the Celtic, Scandinavian, and Germanic tribes)[9] and that of their even earlier ancestors, the Proto-Indo-European Aryans.[10]

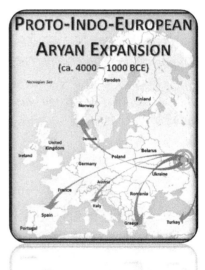

Fra. I:.N:. strongly believed (and passed that belief onto me), that our deepest, most innermost and meaningful spiritual experiences, as well as the keys to unlocking their mysteries, are inherently linked to our knowledge of ourselves, our ancestors, and our cultural heritage.[11] This eternal principle, he would point out, is embedded within Wagner's *Parsifal*, allegorized within the

Hermetic text *Pistis Sophia* or the Christian parable of the Prodigal Son, shadowed within and echoed throughout the lectures of a masonic lodge, and even portrayed and cinematized as part of Neo's introduction to the Oracle or Luke Skywalker's training under Yoda.[12]

In addition to Fra. I:.N:.'s parallel instruction on modern metagenetics and DNA gnosticism,[13] to "know thyself" has been a vital element in the spiritual training of aspiring priests and clerics since antiquity. The ancients were astutely aware of the significance which past events, and one's responses and actions to them, had in providing insight into the aspirant's ministerial forte. These ancients recognized and taught that one's experiences of "self-healing" both provided and indicated the arena in which one would discover and develop their specific niche in the service and healing of others.[14]

Adamantly emphasized in modern Ministry programs as well, within just weeks after beginning my graduate studies I had been assigned the Spiritual Transformation Inventory (STI), the Myers-Briggs Type Indicator (MBTI), the Strong Interest Inventory (SII), the Spiritual Gifts Inventory, and the DVC Learning Styles Inventory. Expressed within such formal academic settings however, the admonishment to know one's self

3

does not typically stem from an attitude eager to foster celebration in one's spiritual victories. Contemporary factors for the administering of these inventories include: 1) the necessity for clergy to have a realistic view of their strengths and limitations so that they might accurately focus their efforts to the betterment of their ministerial community; and 2) to prevent the unconscious influence of the clergy's own experiences, preconceptions, stereotypes and prejudices to be projected upon individual community members.[15]

Donald Tyson, author of *New Millennium Magic: A Complete System of Self-Realization,* summarizes his thought on self-knowledge for every individual, clergy or laity, when he writes:

> Only through self-knowledge—needs, desires, limitations, and abilities—and by being receptive to the guidance of the light can the magus hope with reasonable confidence to tread the single true way of his or her life. This is the esoteric Tao of Chinese philosophy, always unique yet always perfectly suited to each individual.[16]

The path of Asatru is a path to the Source which traverses the most Northern route, cleared and marked specifically for the European psyche. It is a path traveled by our Initiator Odin Himself and then revealed to us by Him as a journey distinguished by one's self-discovery and self-awareness of, self-celebration in, and eventual self-sacrifice to one's Self.

Those who travel the path of Asatru as Einherjar—or, as Edred Thorsson might refer to them as, modern day "operative runologist"—

> …must first and foremost be dedicated to the development of the self—of the very capacity or ability to do magic. This development consists of three components, the internalization of three things: staves, myths, and culture. The meanings and very living essence of each of the rune staves must be absorbed into one's very being. The myths must likewise be synthesized into one's being. Finally, the general underlying cultural principles which eternally give shape to our mysteries must be understood and absorbed. This is a process which requires time and considerable effort. But without it operative runology is difficult to effect.[17]

In *Einherjar—Gnostic Warriors of the North: Way of the Einherjar, Vol. 1*, there are twelve short chapters which are meant to facilitate further conversation and study with a thirteenth chapter meant to serve as a full year's journaling exercise.

The discussion chapters, as mentioned, are brief, blog length chapters (typically 4-6 pages in length) meant to facilitate further discussion. One might choose to read through these chapters in a single session to obtain a general knowledge of the subject matter; or, they may choose to complement these first twelve chapters with that of the journaling exercises of chapter thirteen for a much deeper level of study.

When using the material as a full year's study plan, whether individually or in a group setting, one simply needs to focus on a chapter each month (reading through the chapter at least once per week) while following the journaling schedule provided. Each month should also be spent reading works topically related to that chapter's discussion (the Appendix contains a topical listing of the works cited throughout this entire book).

Einherjar—Gnostic Warriors of the North: Way of the Einherjar, Vol. 1, is a work of applied ancient and modern psychology for assisting contemporary Asatruar along their Path of Return. The material presented, and the manner in which it is presented, is intended for the Spiritual Warrior—one who possesses the courage to take sole responsibility for their spiritual growth and healing as commanders of themselves. It is the hope of this book's author that it and its subject matter will promote spiritual healing through educational empowerment and cultural awareness to all who would read it.

CHAPTER ONE
The European Collective Unconscious

It was not in Wotan's nature to linger on and show signs of old age. He simply disappeared when the times turned against him, and remained invisible for more than a thousand years, working anonymously and indirectly. Archetypes are like riverbeds which dry up when the water deserts them, but which it can find again at any time. An archetype is like an old watercourse along which the water of life has flowed for centuries, digging a deep channel for itself. The longer it has flowed in this channel the more likely it is that sooner or later the water will return to its old bed.

—Carl Jung[18]

Most Asatruar are familiar with Jung's essay. Unfortunately, the significance of his words is often forgotten, unrecognized, or intentionally ignored. Typically, the wisdom of these statements is not given due consideration either because of propagandized associations with WWII Nazi Germany; or, our Folk's lack of appreciation for or ability to apply the metaphysical, psychological, philosophical, and mystical elements at the core of our religious movement and European worldview.

7

The Diversion

Addressing the argument above that the wisdom in Dr. Jung's statements somehow becomes lessened, invalid, or even negated because of its propagandized association with historical events or some political agenda—while there are indeed those who would intentionally propagate and have you believe such a thing—I would like to politely point out that such reasoning and conclusion would be incorrect. Such a conclusion, in fact, neither equates to a sound or valid argument nor does it constitute an argument at all. What is offered here is a very subtle and often unrecognized fallacy in logical reasoning known as a "red-herring."

This "red-herring," as its designation implies, is nothing more than a device intended to create distraction and diversion from the original problem discussed by Dr. Jung—that of the spiritual vacuum within the European psyche.

The truths discussed within Jung's essay continue to be true for the European psyche today, just as they do for the spiritual health of any people and culture, despite any actions having been taken, or which might be taken on behalf of some political agenda. The one has no real effect on the truth of the other.

Assimilation vs Reclamation

A lack of emphasis of, and subsequent lack of appreciation for the metaphysical, psychological, philosophical, and mystical elements fundamental to and at the very core of the religion of Asatru and the European worldview is typically the conscious choice of leaders and practitioners who fear either the semblance of their work to Christianity or the Neo-pagan religion of Wicca.

In the first case, I find it a bit contradictory that during the seasonal "Christian" holidays like Christmas and Easter Asatruar love to remind Christians that those holidays originally belonged to the indigenous heathens of Europe as Yule and Ostara; yet, those same Asatruar, like ritual police (a concept foreign to Asatru Folk by the way), criticize others for similarities between Christian and Asatru ceremonies, customs, practices, and even theological concepts, ideas, or principles.

If "It" was ours first, then logic dictates to me that perhaps Asatruar are not assimilating Christianity into their ceremonies, they may be simply taking back what was theirs in the first place. If restoring the spirituality taken from us by Christianity in its fullest is not the mission, then what are we "re"-constructing?

When I first encountered Asatru and the Asatru Folk movement there was a simple and very fundamental dividing line between heathenry and paganism—while both practiced polytheism and magic, one focused on ancestral worship and one did not. Though this may seem as an over-simplification of the differences by some, it was used for a sound and thoughtful reason.

Modern Wicca, a conglomerate of teachings and practices which Gerald Gardner merged from Freemasonry, Rosicrucianism, Theosophy, Germanic occult societies, etc., like Christianity, is therefore inherently bound to have similarities between its practices and theology with Asatru, for, again like Christianity, they have both borrowed from pre-Christian Europe philosophies, rites and rituals.

The knee-jerk-reaction by Asatruar of either criticizing or avoiding anything metaphysical, philosophical, and mystical because of its appearance of "assimilating" Christianity or Wicca into Asatru rituals or its belief structure needs to be measured and weighed against the reality that in either case it may simply be a matter of reclamation and not assimilation—of which the scholarly may readily know the difference.

The Sounding of Gjallarhorn

As if coordinated and overseen by some eternal and etheric watchman, the restoration of Asatru in the twentieth century is seen by many of its followers as a significant event in the spiritual evolution and healing of the European Folk. Stephen McNallen, in fact, once wrote:

> The rebirth of Asatru was accompanied by an intriguing synchronicity. In England and Iceland, Canada and the United States, four organizations dedicated to the religion of our ancestors were founded within a few months of each other. None knew of the others' existence at the time; only later did they establish communication. A wind was blowing through the branches of the World Tree, marking a new chapter in the evolving saga of the European peoples.[19]

Since being placed on the table of modern religious options in the early 1970s, Asatru has experienced a significant increase in both interest and membership.[20]

Asatru—Religion of the Æsir

Ásatrú—an Icelandic translation of the Swedish word *Asatro* and the Danish word *Asetro*— is a compound word literally translated as "of the gods" (Ása) and "faith," "belief," "religion," or "creed" (-trú).[21] In his book, *A Book of Troth*, Edred Thorsson gives an excellent etymology of the word *Trú*—emphasizing the idea and concept behind the word as a truth based on the trust in one's acquired personal experience "in and of" the gods rather than truth based on external authority.[22] It is from Thorsson's explanation of the word that *Asatru* has taken on its most common translation as "true to the gods."[23]

In literary and linguistic terms, however, Mr. Thorsson's emphasizing of the idea or concept behind the word to produce his translation amounts to what should be properly termed an

amplified or paraphrased "interpretation" of the term and not an actual and literal "translation" of the word and subsequent phrase.

Accordingly, while the word *Asa* does mean "of the gods," it should be remembered that the word is also in its *possessive* case.[24] Therefore, when interpreting the word *Asa* it should be understood to mean "of the god's," and not simply "of the gods," in reference to the term "tru," again meaning "faith," "belief," "creed," or "religion".

The significance of this more literal translation can be seen by comparing and contrasting phrases like: "true to the Asa," with

12

"the Aesir's truth," or, "I have faith in the Aesir," with "I practice the Aesir's faith." Understanding this, to me, has always made a significant difference in my spiritual attitude.

Imagine the influence of a group-soul which thought of itself as the proprietor, practitioner, and propagator of "the god's religion." In fact, this idea of practicing "the god's religion" should not seem like such an odd thought. After all, adhering to a particular religion typically carries with it the intention of following the examples, lessons, teachings, and traditions of one's gods or heroes, adopting their ethics, morals, virtues, ideals and principles as one's own. In effect, practiced as intended, all religions should see themselves as perpetuators of their own god's religion.

To say that practitioners of Asatru follow "the god's religion" also takes on a very metaphysical significance as well, given that the Mysteries of Asatru are not to be found in the life events, adventures or dogma of a single person or system. The Mysteries of Asatru, rather, because they are contained in the sacred myths, are what Joseph Campbell would refer to as penultimate truth—

> ...penultimate because the ultimate cannot be put into words. It is beyond words, beyond images, beyond that bounding rim of the Buddhist Wheel of Becoming. Mythology

pitches the mind beyond that rim, to what can be known but not told. So this is the penultimate truth.[25]

Mr. Campbell continues, emphasizing the experience, knowledge, and benefit gained from such truth, by writing:

It's important to live life with the experience, and therefore the knowledge, of its mystery and of your own mystery. This gives life a new radiance, a new harmony, a new splendor. Thinking in mythological terms helps to put you in accord with the inevitables of this vale of tears. You learn to recognize the positive values in what appear to be the negative moments and aspects of your life. The big question is whether you are going to be able to say a hearty yes to your adventure.[26]

Wotan's reawakening and todays practice of "the religion of the Aesir" is not the creation of human intellect rooted in some physical plain agenda. Asatru is a religious and spiritual movement stemming from the very collective subconscious of the European peoples; and, as Dr. Jung continued to stress in his essay: "all human control comes to an end when the individual is caught in a mass movement. Then, the archetypes begin to function…."[27]

CHAPTER TWO
Way of the Einherjar

Thus, in the course of uncounted generations all men will become Einherjar, and that state-willed and preordained by the godhead-of general liberty, equality, and fraternity will be reached. This is that state which sociologists long for and which socialists want to bring about by false means, for they are not able to comprehend the esoteric concept that lies hidden in the triad: liberty, equality, fraternity, a concept which must first ripen and mature in order that someday it can be picked like a fruit from the World Tree.

—Guido von List

Warrior-Monk

One of my favorite movies is Sturla Gunnarsson's 2005 film, *Beowulf & Grendel.* Though some elements of the film were only loosely based on the original poem, I applaud Gunnarsson, nonetheless, for his movie's thought provoking and psychological elements in its portrayal of Beowulf as the "warrior-monk" archetype.[28]

When Beowulf first appears in the film he seeks only to kill a monster. Throughout the film, Beowulf and his men are faced with ordeals and opportunities to honor their oaths, prove their boasts, and, at times, to even validate their noble progress toward greater Self-awareness and self-mastery. By the time of his departure, having fulfilled his mission without regret, Beowulf leaves with a newly found respect for his deceased adversary and a profound awareness of his effect on the tapestry of wyrd and the cycles of life.

Spiritual-Warrior

In contrast to Gunnarsson's film—yet in the same sense of seeing a warrior from an unfamiliar perspective due to cultural stereotypes—is the 1996 American film, *Michael*, starring John Travolta and Andie MacDowell.[29] Making an entrance in the film and first impression on his guests in the story like only an archangel could do, Michael lackadaisically makes his way downstairs dressed in just his boxer shorts. Smoking a cigarette, Michael then stops in the living room on his way to the refrigerator for an ice-cold morning beer to scratch his man-parts and greet his guests.

Notwithstanding the comedic entertainment of the film, a significant point is made by Michael to Ms. Winters, the resident "angel expert" played by Andie MacDowell. Ms. Winters and her companions expected "halos" and "inner light" from Michael, but instead they were confronted by a seasoned warrior.

Forgotten by Ms. Winters was that—like the Greek god Mars, the Roman god Ares, and the Norse god Tyr—the archangel Michael, though "guardian of righteousness and justice", also assumes the post and office of Commander of Heaven's Army and, by default, the archetype of a "god of war." Michael's audience was taken aback by his actions because they didn't understand the true nature behind Michael and his mission, and to this Michael could only respond with the sincere and divine truth— "I'm not that kind of angel."

Initiate-Knight

To limit such influences of urban legend,[30] consideration of our topic is given first to the historical Einherjar. It will then be shown from the Norse myths regarding their journey to Valhalla and their post as guardians of Bifrost that numerous literary symbols resemble those of known systems of wisdom training and progressive, initiatory instruction.

It should be noted here however that this is not to imply or promote the idea that herein lies a Teutonic pantheon overlaid upon some Hermetic or K/C/Qabalistic glyph.[31] While such practice is good for just that—practice—and has its place in what is properly called "the outer lodge," any valid "Aquarian-age" Teutonic Mystery School—while utilizing many of the contemporary principles of Jungian Psychology and ancient techniques of instruction, ritual, and guided meditation—must also recognize the importance of and vital role that one's family history, ancestral memory and even their DNA plays in the study, practice, and application of The Craft.[32]

Lodges of the Northern Mysteries forsake the grand mission and purpose of their charter if they fail to properly address the psyche of an Odinic Consciousness within the initiatory system they promote.

Combining contemporary studies with principles of ancient wisdom aids in preventing subjective interpretations of the mythos under examination, as well demonstrates the hidden knowledge possessed by the ancients within their archaic, mystical, and symbolic language.

CHAPTER THREE
Religious Education and Asatru

Religious concepts originally had relevance and continue to have relevance only when they relate to human experience…. Progression in learning is achieved by analyzing concepts into their constituent parts and then systematically exploring the different parts of the main concept at different stages of the pupils' education. The pupil builds up an increasingly conceptual grid of religious doctrine, through which a proper understanding of religion will be realized.

—L. P. Barnes[33]

While sorting through and organizing years of material to be considered for inclusion in our kindred's formal Asatruar religious education and study program, I came across three particularly outstanding comments by Stephen McNallen, founder of one of the foremost Asatru organizations in North America, which were both applicable to the given program development project as well as particularly suited to the demographics of our kindred and any future initiates which might be considered for kindred membership.

New Millennium Objectives

At the turn of the 21st century Mr. McNallen wrote:

We have not made a systematic effort to bring in more or less ordinary people—those looking for ancestral European roots, for fellowship with their own kind, for a sacralized vision of the world, or simply for a way to live good and rewarding lives. Asatru has the spiritual power to recruit educated, financially successful men and women with functioning lives, if only we present it properly. It is time to tailor our message to this end…. we need to reach out to young families, college students, business executives, and the creative thinkers who shape our world.[34]

Mr. McNallen also emphasized, referencing Alain de Benoist's writings, that contemporary Asatru Folk:

[C]annot ignore the fact that Christianity has dominated us for more than a millennium. It is an error to think that we can simply pick up where we left off a thousand years ago. The Christian interregnum must be addressed, using the intellectual tools that have developed in the intervening time— and this means examining our beliefs and expressing them in intellectually compelling ways.[35]

And, over a decade after first making these statements, Mr. McNallen remained confident that Asatru must reach beyond its usual target audience to the public at large if it is to ever become more than "a tiny cult on the fringe of American life."[36]

New Millennium Approach

Merging these admonishments into the design of our kindred's curriculum, it was decided that a minimum of three points needed to be addressed.

First and foremost, the cornerstone of our kindred curriculum should be the spiritual healing and growth of those sincerely desiring to return to their ancient ancestral European roots.

Second, while moving us toward a greater understanding of our European ancestors and the "old ways" of our ancient folk religion, our curriculum should also guard against and inherently address the problem of "throwing out the baby with the bath water," as it were, in regard to the "Christian interregnum."

Our kindred, for instance, recognizes that while witchcraft, sorcery, and magic were eventually outlawed by "the church," the fact remains that occult teachings were never destroyed or extinguished, they simply became the sole possession of the authorized religious authority.[37]

Similarly, meditation techniques, relaxation exercises, and mystical methods of obtaining union with the divine were never lost or forgotten by the ancients, their use was simply disallowed by any religion other than the state religion of Christianity and its appointed priests.[38] Even today, the use of visualization, mantras, guided meditation, and even sympathetic magic is employed within such Christian exercises as praying the rosary, meditating on the icon cards, or walking the Stations of the Cross.

Magic and Meditation were practiced as spiritual exercises and rituals throughout Europe long before the Jewish schism which became Christianity ever occurred. These ideas and processes must not be overlooked because they have been tarnished; but, they must be reverently polished so they may once again adorn our temples and edify our Folk.

The last leg of our curriculum deals directly with the topic of Religious Education itself. Just because disciplines such as textural criticism, hermeneutics, church planting, evangelism, fundraising, pastoral counseling, etc. have been fine-tuned behind the doors of Christian seminaries, the value and use of such research and development should not be ignored, discarded or discouraged as Asatru seeks to enlarge its footprint in today's spiritual sector. Instead, "magically" applying the formula, *Solve et Coagula*, such practices should be adapted for and utilized in our own local reconstruction efforts.

CHAPTER FOUR
Modern Psychology and Ancient Wisdom

The tree forms another connecting link between the mind of the magician and events in the world. The key to accessing this flow of information is to realize—to make real—the fullness of the tree within the individual's hyperbody (or psyche). Then those parts of the hyperbody which correspond to parts in the cosmos—or more correctly actually resonate with them—can be stimulated to cause changes in the outer world. Once this state is achieved, the absolute distinctions between god-man-world can be momentarily dissolved—at which time the individual can act directly on the universe itself....it is in these moments that magic occurs

—Edred Thorsson.[39]

Guardians and The Threshold Concept

Sentinels or "Guardians of the Threshold," as they are often called, are charged with the protection of their mysteries and the initiatory secrets associated with their particular approach to the "Source". Such guardians, like those upon the journey to Valhalla, may guard the initial entrance upon the journey, the entrance to various stages along that journey, or the final entrance to the destined hall itself. Such entities act as either "guardians" against entry by the unworthy on the one hand or "portals" to higher consciousness for the chosen on the other.[40] Though an ancient device often described in a mythical, mystical fashion, these Guardians of the Threshold do represent an actual psychological form or archetype known to us today as a *threshold concept*.[41]

Like an encounter with a Guardian of the Threshold as described within the archives of many mystery schools and pages of esoteric literature, an encounter with a Threshold Concept is described as being Troublesome, Irreversible, Integrative, Bounded, and Transformative:[42]

- As a Troublesome entity, these concepts and the light they bear are not easily understood or comprehended, first appearing as other-worldly, culturally alien, and even illogical to the individual confronted by this grotesque and deformed figure.

- Once they are adequately considered and gradually understood, these troublesome concepts and the knowledge they yield is not easily unlearned and is, very likely, as Irreversible as the un-ringing of a bell or the un-thinking of a thought.

☀ Now, rather than a conglomerate of disjointed and randomly forced together contradictive components, the Threshold Concept becomes an Integrative image that equips the individual with the ability to interweave previously assumed dissimilar aspects of the larger picture.

☀ Instead of being comprised of opposing forces, as initially thought by the seeker, the various elements that make up the Threshold Concept are seen as being actually Bounded together, forming and defining within itself a complementary system of academic fields, disciplinary areas, and even study subjects and topics.

☀ Ultimately, the thought process that occurs as a result of coming to an understanding of, appreciation for, and mastery over the Threshold Concept, like an encounter with a Guardian of the Threshold, is so Transformative and life altering that it significantly effects the way the individual now views the particular discipline, themselves, and even the world around them.[43]

To demonstrate how a Threshold Concept or Guardian manifests itself on this plain, let me offer two contrasting examples. For my first example let me tell you about this group of Christians who walked out of a graduate class during the airing of the PBS documentary *From Jesus to Christ*.[44] To this small group of classmates it was unthinkable that "Jesus of Nazareth" might actually have been born in Nazareth rather than Bethlehem, as is suggested during the documentary. Their inability to separate the historical Jesus from the mythical Logos or the mystical Christ proved they were not ready for the knowledge they had asked to receive. In this case the Threshold Concept never progressed beyond that Troublesome and illogical entity, subsequently causing it to assume the role of Guardian and roadblock. Acting as a psychological survival mechanism, protecting the dogmatic worldview of these students from total collapse, the Guardian denied them further access along this particular path.

The other example which I have personally observed over the years comes from the adaptation of mystical tools into one's ritual life to achieve spiritual growth. While I could choose from a number of "magical weapons" to demonstrate the process, the best example naturally comes from the most controversial among Heathen, Pagan, and Christian circles alike—A. E. Waite's Tarot.

Particular to those on a Northern path, the Tarot is usually avoided due to: 1) the belief that symbols in the deck are too "Christian," and/or 2) the belief that the idea of a tarot deck was not known to the ancient indigenous European tribes.

It has been my good fortune however, to have witnessed heathens who have had the courage to test the mettle of their preconceptions.

Once some time was spent in tarot studies, these courageous few came to recognize and appreciate its ancient pre-Christian symbolic meanings;[45] through even temporary use of the tarot aspirants quickly and accurately learned to relate to the runes as they were before the transitional period (c. 500 CE)—when the runes were viewed as symbols and images rather than letters, resembling in effect the idea behind today's tarot deck more than an actual alphabet;[46] and, the seeker soon came to a deeper understanding and appreciation of the ancient and modern works which remind us of the true origins of subjects like the Kabalah.[47]

This particular Guardian of the Threshold and Threshold Concept eventually became for these students that final Bounding agent and subsequent portal for instruction and training in the Odinic Mysteries, not as a substitute for or even an adaptation to their regular Asatru and runic practices and studies; but, as a preliminary psychological training aid for effectively improving communication skills with one's subconscious.

What was once seen as a barrier and obstacle between them and their Northern tradition became, as if by magic, a portal for better and deeper understanding and application of the Mysteries of Asatru, the Magic of Operant Runology, and the Wisdom of Esoteric Runosophy.

Psychological Mapping and The Cube

Use of a cube to explain the human psyche is an ancient technique most commonly associated with the Kabalistic book *The Sefer Yetzirah* and its descriptions of the dimensions of consciousness.[48] The Cube is also associated with The Philosopher's Stone of Alchemy[49] and the Perfect Ashtar of Freemasonry.

The Cube as Symbol of Perfection

According to Albert Pike, author of *Morals and Dogma of the Ancient and Accepted Scottish Rite of Freemasonry*:

> If we delineate a cube on a plane surface thus: we have visible three faces, and nine external lines, drawn between seven points. The complete cube has three more faces, making six; three more lines, making twelve; and one more point, making eight. As the number 12 includes the sacred numbers, 3, 5, 7, and 3 times 3, or 9, and is produced by adding the sacred number 3 to 9; while its own two figures, 1, 2, the unit or monad, and duad, added together, make the same sacred number 3; it was called the perfect number; and the cube became the symbol of perfection.[50]

The cube is often used as a linguistic symbol to represent or emphasize the concept and idea of perfection. Many people are familiar with but fail to see the

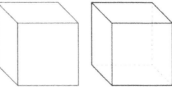

significance in the cubical structures of biblical text. For instance, consider the meeting tent of Moses which housed the Ark of the Covenant, measuring 15'x15'x15'; the Holy of Holy of Solomon's temple, which was 30'x30'x30'; and the Heavenly Jerusalem in The Revelation, which is recorded as having walls that measure 14,000 miles wide, 14,000 miles deep, and 14,000 miles high.[51]

The Three Planes and Dimensions

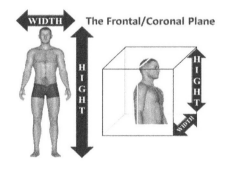

The Frontal/Coronal Plane

The Frontal or Coronal Plane is made up of hight and width. It is equivalent to looking at a two dimensional image, like looking at a square rather than a cube. We might hear of a very "two-dimensional" subject or person as being shallow or having no depth, which is such a precise observation that it is concidered a vocal reference and linguistic cue by some of our subconscious recognition of the concept of psychological space and psycho-spatial orientation.[52] This is considered the Plane of Existence and its energy extends from the top to the bottom of the cube, forming a relationship between the opposing forces of material vs. spiritual goals..[53]

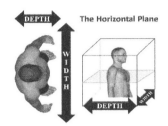

The Horizontal Plane adds depth to width and is parallel to the base and top of the cube. This is considered the Plane of Interpretation—connecting the right and left, perception and sensation sides of the cube.

Finally, adding depth to hight gives us what is called the Saggital Plane. This plane is considered the Plane of Life and adds the element of time to our

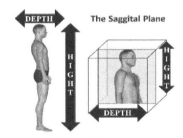

consideration of space, illustrating the relationship between the future and the past, that which is before us and yet to be experienced with that which is behind us and has already been experienced.

The Seven Sides and Directions

When we consider a cube we usually consider its six sides or directions (top, bottom, front, back, left, and right), but what do we mean by a seven sided cube? Consider if you will once again the previously mentioned linguistic symbols—the tabinacle of Moses, the Holy of Holies of Solomon's temple, and the New or Heavenly Jerusalem—and note that each of these structures would be considered incomplete if not for the article located at its center.

The significance of this seventh direction, the center, is also highlighted symbolically in the Genesis creation story. Genesis 1 describes the first six days of creation, or first six sides of the

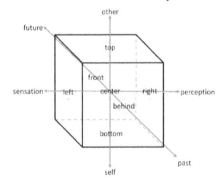

cube. It is on the seventh day, in Genesis 2, that God is said to have rested, making this the day that was to be kept holy.[54] The center of the cube, its seventh side, structurally or symbolically,

is always presented as the seat of holiness (even in "non-pagan," "non-heathen" literature!).

The Twelve Edges

The twelve edges of the cube are often associated with several various categories of correspondences. Physio-psychologically the twelve edges are typically associated with organic actions or the organs of the body. Organic actions would include the five senses, nutrition, exercise, and emotional responses. The organs of the body most often associated with the edges of the cube are the hands, feet, kidneys, liver, stomach, intestines, the spleen, bile, and maw.[55] Other tables of correspondences for the twelve edges might include the months of the year, the zodiac, or even the influences of the twelve halls of Asgard.

The Four Diagonals and Eight Corners

The ancient Hellenistic school of Stoic philosophy taught that the soul consisted of eight different components, collectively called the *hêgemonikon*. These eight components originated within the *hêgemonikon* and were considered to be spatial extensions or emanations of the *pneuma*, the vital spirit or creative force of each person. The eight parts of the *hêgemonikon* are the five senses, the reproductive faculty, the speech faculty, and the central commanding faculty [also called a *hêgemonikon*].

In addition to the eight spatial parts of the soul described in Stoic philosophy, the human *hêgemonikon* was also characterized by four powers: impulse [*hormê*], assent [*sugkatathesis*], presentation [*phantasia*], and reason [*logos*].[56]

Mapping this Hellenistic idea of the psyche or soul on our cube, we find the *pneuma*, its vital creative spirit, at its center emanating or extending itself as eight spatially distinct entities, the cube's corners. The emanation of the *pneuma* as these eight parts of the soul occurs through and by way of the four powers associated with the *hêgemonikon*, identified in our mapping as the four diagonals of the cube and eight "legs" or directions of the *pneuma*.

The Norse Psycho-Cosmological Cube

Merging the ancient principles of mapping which we have discussed with modern descriptions of the Norse psyche detailed within Edred Thorsson's studies and published writings produces a perfect psycho-cosmological image which we, like initiates of various other mystery schools and traditions, can utilize for meditation, contemplation, and our own self-discovery.[57]

According to Mr. Thorsson, there are nine fundamental Nordic psychological constructs which constitute the "whole man": the physical body (Lik); the etheric matrix of the physical body (Hamr); the mystical- or astral-self called "the fetch" (Fylgja); that component of the self which allows for the experience of mystical ecstasy (Odhr); one's "luck" (Hamingja); memory

(Minni); the logical mind (Hugr); the shade, or "shadow" as Jung would call it (Sal); and, at the center of it all, located in the same honored place as the Indian *prana*, the Sanskrit *atman*, and the Greek *pneuma*, one's vital energy and breath, the Divine spark (Ond).[58]

This Nordic model uses all the components of the cube—three dimensions, eight directions/sides plus the center, all the edges, and even the corners.[59] This is a perfect image of the Divine spark and vital energy emanating throughout the three dimensions and the eight directions. Our model clearly depicts the nine worlds and eight legs of Yggdrasil, making real, as it were, "the fullness of the tree within the individual's hyperbody (or psyche)."[60]

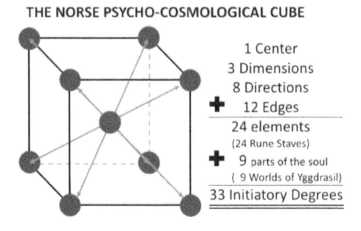

THE NORSE PSYCHO-COSMOLOGICAL CUBE

1 Center
3 Dimensions
8 Directions
✚ 12 Edges
_____
24 elements
(24 Rune Staves)
✚ 9 parts of the soul
(9 Worlds of Yggdrasil)
33 Initiatory Degrees

CHAPTER FIVE
Theory and Philosophy of Religion

According to Vedanta cosmology, under Brahman fall relatively Lesser Realities which the other religions of the world confess as their God or gods. Since even these Lesser Realities are true emanations from the Highest Reality (Brahman), all religions may be said to, in essence, worship the same Object, Brahman.

—Scott David Foutz[61]

When considering the theory and philosophy of religion, a student should become familiar with at least the three main theories of Animism, Humanism and the Astral Theory, as well as the accompanying concept of Otto's *sensus numinus*.[62]

Animism

According to the theory of animism ancient peoples, in their earliest stages of development, given that it is a human characteristic to think that everyone and everything must "think" as we do, attributed a form of human personality—with all of its emotion, cognizance, ego, and ambitions—to every object in nature.[63] Subsequently, since nature and its component parts possessed their own personality, or spirit, it was accepted that such could also mindfully, willingly, intentionally, and subjectively effect, either for the recipients' benefit or detriment, the lives of those that they came into contact with.

Additionally, just as these early humans could please or anger other humans, it would have been considered reasonable for them to believe that they could also please or anger nature and its spirits as well. Over time, as this theory proposes, humankind would come to eventually look upon nature, its spirits and its gods with "active reverence and propitiation."[64]

Examined in light of modern psychology, these early humans, who undoubtedly harbored feelings of anxiety due to their sense of dependence upon nature's whims, or the god's moods as they probably saw it, would naturally be expected to exhibit such overt and clinical signs of "projection."[65] This tendency to project human characteristics and personality traits upon various objects, when considered within an academic setting, is referred to as anthropomorphism.[66]

For purposes of discussion within the discipline of philosophy of religion, anthropomorphism refers specifically to the assigning of human attributes to god/the gods.[67] Bringing this train of thought forward and to its logical conclusion, Ludwig Feuerbach, a nineteenth century German philosopher, claimed that all theology should be recognized as being anthropology and all religion should be recognized as anthropomorphic, since god is fundamentally viewed as being "a projection of unfulfilled human potential."[68]

Though the theory of animism allows for an individual's conscious awareness of his or her own personality, and the projection of that personality upon other objects, the theory itself admits that it does not account for the subsequent worshipping of such personalities or for the development of the act of worship proper within the idea of religion.

The Sensus Numinus

To account for this religious element of worship within animism the concept of a *sensus numinus*, or *mystical sense*, within all of humankind must be accepted.[69] This sensus numinus, according to the German theologian and scholar of comparative religion Rudolf Otto, is an innate sense, operating independently of any typical biological sense perception, of the divine which has been deeply implanted within the human psyche.[70]

For Otto, the sensus numinus is distributed evenly to all humankind and is the only source of any religious perception.[71] Subsequently, in line with Otto's philosophy and as an extended element of the theory of animism, the divine is not seen as revealing itself to humanity, but it is through the sensus numinus that humankind becomes aware of the divine.[72] It is this sensus numinus then that accounts for the development of worship within the theory of animism.

Humanism

Humanism is the modern term for an ancient theory on the origin of religion claimed to be based on the views of Sicilian writer Euhēmeros (c. 315 BCE).[73] According to Euhēmeros and his theory, all the gods were simply humans who had died and been deified because of their worthy deeds and noble character.[74] Following the "common sense" tendency of his time, Euhēmeros considered the ancient myths and tales of the gods to be mere exaggerations of the facts and historical events put into poetic verse and terms of the miraculous.[75]

Seen by some as an inherent issue within this same theory, we find that not every human who died was believed to have become a god and not all gods were considered to have once been human.[76] Within the structure of this theory there was a distinct difference between gods that were gods by nature and gods who were gods due to human achievement, advancement, and their acquisition of "the mode of being of the gods."[77] In fact, the ancients had three separate designations for their gods—there were the gods that represented natural forces, there were the gods that the poets wrote of, and there were the gods celebrated through the state religion.[78]

The Astral Theory

The Astral Theory supposes that religion originated from humanity's worship of the heavenly bodies. Inherent in this theory, like animism, there needs to be the presupposition of the sensus numinus. "Religion," which in this case would be understood as the veneration of the planets and stars, is impossible to explain in the absents of this sensus numinus, just as the science of optics would be impossible without the sense of sight.[79]

According to the gnostic text *Poimandres*. God created the *nous* (mind, intelligence) which in turn created (physical) nature. Subsequently, each person consists of a body (from nature) which imprisons the soul (from God).

To achieve deification (salvation from the body and deliverance from the oppressive fate of the stars) an individual needed to gain knowledge (gnosis) of natural and metaphysical laws. Reception of this gnosis is described in Hermetic and Gnostic text as the rebirth; and, with this gnosis the faithful Hermetic hoped to ascend past the seven astral spheres and to reunite with God (the Source and Center of Consciousness).[80]

Dionysius divided the gods into three categories. The first category included what he thought were the most obvious, i.e. the Sun, Moon, and Stars. Next, he lists those which are not apparent but are typically associated with natural forces like Neptune, god of the sea. The third group then included those which were said to have passed from the human state to the divine, as Hercules and Amphiaraus.

Where we read of heavenly guard-houses and posts or watchmen within gnostic text, the reference is typically directed at either a planet or the supposed guardian of that sphere. For instance, the Hermetic text *Pistis Sophia,* gives an excellent description of the path of the soul going past guard-houses blocking the access to heaven.[81]

CHAPTER SIX
From Homosapian to Homospiritus

To enter into the divine nature is equivalent to attaining divinity
—Dionysus[82]

The intent of one's indoctrination into an ancient mystery school and initiation in gnostic philosophy was to promote and facilitate a progressive development of the participant's levels of consciousness and character in preparation for future service.

Using the typical literary symbolism of the day, this raising of the levels of consciousness by the initiate and the subsequent developing of the virtuous warrior was often referred to in alchemical terms as "squaring the circle" or the "turning of lead," a base metal, "into gold," the most precious of metals. This process was also referred to or allegorized in many religious belief systems as: the path of return (i.e. to the Source of consciousness); coming to "know thyself"; approach to the Sanctum Sanctorum; the experience of atonement [ultimate union and communication] with the Divine; the Solar-Lunar conjunction; and, the Hieros Gamos (Gk. *Sacred Marriage*).

The Process of Human Change

"Know Thyself," a concept taught by Socrates to his students, printed over the entrances of ancient temples, and quoted often by counselors and psychologists today has had such an influence upon human change in the areas of sociology, politics, science, and religion that neither its philosophical nor psychological implications should be ignored.

The process of human change, whether the subject of change is a complete society or a single individual, begins as soon as the subject is made the focus of observation. Historically, as soon as humankind came to understand what it meant to be human there occurred immediate and natural changes in the way people related to others within the society in which they lived. Subsequently changes also took place in the accepted social norms of the day regarding cultural mannerisms and the treatment of others. As individuals came to understand themselves—their own feelings, emotions, thoughts, etc.—they could more easily understand others, being able to empathize because of their own self-knowledge and self-healing.[83]

Achieving the Good Life

Socrates believed that it was essential for individuals to understand themselves in order for them to achieve what he referred to as "the good life". This achievement of the good life, according to Socrates, had nothing to do with the acquisition of wealth or power, but was defined by one's ethics, virtue, and the treatment of others. The extent to which one gained knowledge of self was directly proportional to one's ability to demonstrate such ethics among their fellow citizens. For Socrates and his contemporaries living an ethical life was living the good life.[84]

"Living" the Good Life

Ultimately, this process of human change would have a direct impact on the degree to which one would experience and exhibit the good life. The more individuals came to know themselves and to understand the process of human development and growth, acknowledging the process of human change from infancy to adulthood and the various levels of acceptable social norms at each of these levels of development, the more ethical and virtuous those individuals would act. Less sociable behavior seen among children was explained by Socrates as a result of their ignorance and lack of self-knowledge, while the more socially acceptable actions of adults were explained and attributed to a deeper and greater level of self-knowledge of themselves and their understanding of the functions of their society. Subsequently, the degree to which individuals would experience and exhibit the good life, according to Socrates, was seen as being dependent upon their own level of human growth, their understanding of themselves and the processes of human growth, and the individuals' ability to act accordingly.[85]

Plato and Human Nature

Plato, a student of Socrates, understood human nature as being composed of a body, which collected changing and fallible information from the outer world through its frail senses, and the soul, which revealed the more permanent and reliable world of form through the process of thought and reason.

Using the metaphor of a charioteer to illustrate human nature, Plato saw the body as the outer chariot and the soul as the charioteer who attempts to control the chariot through control of its two opposing forces, symbolized by the two horses which pull the chariot—one horse representing humankinds' animal appetites and passions and the other horse representing humankinds' higher spiritual aspirations and motives.[86]

Plato also illustrated his dualistic understanding of human nature through his Allegory of the Cave. Here Plato illustrated the dualistic nature of the world and humankind by pointing out that there was one understanding of the world devised from the produced shadows which appeared on the cave's wall and a more realistic understanding of the world which was derived from the true reality which occurred outside the cave. Plato defined much of his understanding of the nature of humankind, from love to memory, in light of this Allegory.[87]

Influence of the Unconscious

In every area of life--sports, education, employment, relationships, etc.—understanding where one's strengths and limitations lie is often the key to improvement, growth and ultimately success. The same would seem to hold true when we consider the perspective of psychology which maintains that much, if not all, of what a human thinks, says, or does stems from unconscious influences from within that person.[88]

From a psychological perspective then, it would follow that as one would gain and improve upon their understanding of these influences they should also gain and improve upon their ability to control their thoughts, emotions and behaviors.[89] Additionally, it would also seem to follow that any deficiencies in one's social, learning, and/or behavioral development might stem from their lack of understanding and inability to control these influences of the unconscious mind.[90]

Moral and Ethical Implications

The moral and ethical implications that arise when one considers that humanity, as a whole and as individual entities, has the ability to learn to understand and then control its unconscious impulses—directing its thoughts and actions as social and human evolution dictates—has been the topic of many literary works throughout history.

For centuries human kind has used practices like sleep deprivation, meditation, visualization, the "dream quest" and even voluntarily induced pain to specifically aid in communicating with the subconscious and limiting or emphasizing those unconscious influences behind that behavior pattern they wish to modify. Over time acceptable morals, values and ethics have been redefined as societies and individuals have come to understand, appreciate, and expect that a control over one's actions is not dictated by an uncontrollable unconscious mind.

Implications on Professional and Criminal Behavior

The outward expression of society's acknowledgement and acceptance of this concept—that we are not left to the dictates of our unconscious impulses—can be seen when one considers that the breaking of laws and committing of crimes throughout history has little to do with the so-called offense, but has much more to do with when and where the particular act was conducted. Behavior, for instance, which might have been acceptable centuries ago, might now be forbidden in today's society. Actions currently acceptable in one state or country may, at the same time, be against the law in another state or country. Years ago one could claim uncontrollable passion as an excuse for typically unacceptable behavior under the guise of "temporary insanity." Today, however, statutory laws of many states have been rewritten to redefine their use of such a phrase, holding individuals accountable for their actions in spite of the emotional trauma which they may have experienced.

Similarly, in today's workplace one is expected to be in control of his or her emotions and behaviors at all times. Outbursts of emotion, the raising of one's voice, use of threatening language, or expressions of aggressive behavior are all seen as unacceptable in today's modern workplace and would probably be addressed with some form of disciplinary action. As mentioned above, long gone are the days when "seeing red" can be used as a defense for not maintaining control of one's passions or as an excuse for one's inappropriate social behavior.

Implications on the Process of Human Change

In considering Freud's view on human nature we find that he was a firm believer that the unconscious influenced humans to often act in ways that were defeating and nonproductive;[91] however, like a commentary on the symbolism of the Egyptian Sphinx, Freud also believed that it was within man to learn to overcome these base and animalistic influences and once again become master over his or her own "mental life".[92]

Additionally, Freud believed that consciously or not humankind spent its entire existence seeking pleasure and avoiding pain.[93] It was this bottom line motivation which he believed formed the basis for all human influences behind one's thoughts, speech, and actions.[94]

Because of the unconscious influences that humans contend with, it was Freud's opinion that the whole purpose of psychoanalysis was to widen one's conscious awareness and to subsequently liberate the individual from the harmful influences which were beforehand uncontrollable.[95] In recognizing and subsequently understanding these unconscious influences, i.e. making them now conscious influences, one could come to control and alter them to aid in changing previous behavior patterns.[96]

Understanding the symbols and images often used by the unconscious to communicate to the conscious mind is a task that each individual should undertake to better understand their own limitations and strengths.[97] Since most of our thoughts and actions are governed by these unconscious influences, recognizing and controlling these influences would ultimately amount to one's learning to control their own emotions, passions, and even physical responses.[98]

Learning to control our conscious thoughts and behaviors begins with learning to control those unconscious influences behind the conscious mind.[99] Having such control, however, also makes us responsible and accountable for socially acceptable levels of morality and ethical behavior.[100]

The Goal of Human Change

The concept of the "awakened" or "deified" human was not foreign to the ancients. Not all, but some of the gods were but mere mortals who had died and been deified due to their worthy deeds.[101] The ancient's were said to have known Atlas as a great astronomer associated with the geometric shape of the sphere; thus, his depiction with the sphere of the world set upon his shoulders.[102] Jove's story of his smiting the giants with thunderbolts was recognized as a story of the king responding to acts of treason.[103] Prometheus is said to have been a sculptor, so he is naturally associated with creating humans out of clay.[104] And mighty Zeus himself was said to be the ancient king of Crete, buried on the island in a sepulcher bearing his name.[105]

Of those gods who were gods due to human achievement and advancement, it was said that they had acquired the attitude or "the mode of being of the gods."[106] Plato of Athens wrote that the first thing people would say about their gods was that "they exist by art and not by nature, by certain legal conventions which differ from place to place, according as each tribe agreed when forming their laws."[107]

.

CHAPTER SEVEN
Operant Conditioning and Superstition

The universe constantly "communicates" with the individual through the five senses, but also by what happens to the individual. We experience events or phenomena as received messages from the world. By modifying the transmission by means of the universal encoder—the runes—we may modify what happens.

Edred Thorsson[108]

Throughout time and around the world cultures, societies, tribes, clans, and families have developed traditions which they hold vital to the unity and survival of their group. Such traditions are typically performed and perpetuated for the purpose of warding off some negative influence or calling for the addition of some positive influence for the betterment of the society.[109]

Just as operant conditioning is used within a society for the perpetuation of its traditions and customs, individuals, influenced by perceived "good" and "bad luck", or "punishment" and "blessings", throughout their day come to develop and perpetuate their own set of superstitions. These personally developed superstitions are often used to guide one's daily activities—the individual convinced that his or her success or failure is now dependent upon adherence to earlier behavior.[110]

Operant conditioning is often viewed as the purposeful administration of reinforcement (i.e., consequences that influence reoccurrence of a particular behavior, a reward) or punishment (i.e., consequences that influence the discontinuance of a particular behavior) to influence behavior patterns.[111] There is, however, operant conditioning that occurs on an accidental and random level rather that a purposefully and controlled level. These accidentally developed behavioral patterns are usually referred to as superstitions and typically provide no necessary or useful purpose in the realization of the anticipated consequence.[112]

Historical Antecedents

The operant conditioning theory was first formally researched and presented by E. L. Thorndike after deducing from the behavior of his subjects, a randomly selected group of cats, that behavior which preceded a reward would be repeated and behavior which immediately preceded a less satisfying consequence would be discontinued.[113] Thorndike, however, focused on controlled operant conditioning by demanding that the cats move a rod in order to be fed.[114]

Accidental operant conditioning and the presents of superstition in the behavior of animals, however, were first noticed by B. F. Skinner while experimenting with a group of pigeons. It was during Skinner's research that he happened to notice individual behavioral patterns which had developed among the pigeons just before feeding time, though, unlike Thorndike's cats who needed to move a rod to be feed, no such behavior was necessary or required for the distribution of their food.[115] Skinner realized that whatever behavior each pigeon may have been performing immediately prior to their being feed continued to be exhibited by that pigeon just prior to future feedings, even though that behavior was totally random and had no relevance as to whether the pigeon would receive food or not.[116]

Development of Superstition

Maintenance and development of superstitions among humans occur due to similar circumstances as those which occurred among the pigeons. As noted by Skinner himself, it takes but a few accidental favorable consequences, many after the initial coincidence being self-perpetuating, to establish and maintain a behavior pattern that in truth offers no real effect on the resulting consequences.[117]

Superstitions of the Past

People often find it intriguing to discover that many cathedrals and churches throughout the world are actually built upon ancient spiritual sites, some still containing in the depths of their basements original fragments and runes of ancient alters or burial ground markers.[118] The church of St. Michael in Somerset, England, for example, is built upon Glastonbury Hill, a sacred place that holds connections to ancient Celtic civilizations that believed the hill was actually the doorway to the Kingdom of the Lord of the Underworld.[119] Later years would have the same hill visited by those celebrating the Great Earth Mother and Goddess.[120] Years later the hill is believed to have been used as the location of King Arthur's Avalon.[121] Archeology has also revealed the existence of what could be either a Neolithic maze or a Middle Age designed farmland—or perhaps the topographical lay out of seven symmetrical terraces along the hill's sloping sides were used as both maze and farmland, depending on the century in question.[122]

The belief of spiritual energy being present at this particular location on Earth has played a vital role in the historical events of the people of this area in England. The operant conditioning process that first brought tribes to this site continued to influence those who came afterwards, causing them to perpetuate the earlier conditioned behavior by reestablishing the previous location as the social gathering point for the community by building new churches upon ancient alters.[123]

Getting Past Superstitions

Superstitions can be controlled using the three same elements which control all operant conditioned behaviors—reward, punishment, and extinction.[124]

To bring about the "extinction" of a superstition, a behavior that offers no rational effect on any particular consequence, no action, either positive or negative should be taken as a result of the unwanted behavior. This lack of either reinforcement or punishment will ultimately cause the unwanted behavior to cease.[125]

Tradition and Ritual vs. Superstition

With the acknowledgement and use of metaphysical laws and concepts, it becomes necessary for us to carefully consider what behavior patterns may or may not offer any "real" cause behind a desired and resulting effect. Subsequently, tradition and ritual is differentiated from superstition within The Craft through the eyes of the participant. If a participant in a ritual understands the purpose and intent behind its elements and components, then they can fully participate in the "tradition". If, on the other hand, one participates without any real understanding of the "why" or "what for" behind the ritual—just going through the motions, as it were—then they are seen as non-participants in the tradition and their actions are understood as mere superstition

A tradition in many families of Northern European ancestry is the lighting of the Yule log during the week of winter solstice. Though many families and individuals may participate in the activity, many are unfamiliar with the philosophy and idea behind the lighting of the log and that it is performed for the purpose of attracting the Sun back into the Northern sky from its Southern grave.[126] Fewer still recognize that they celebrate this same tradition, for the same magical intent, even as they adorn yard, home, and temple with candles and lights in review of the passing year and in anticipation of the coming, returning Sun.

CHAPTER EIGHT
The Process of Thinking

The four core processes of social cognition, the process by which all humans "think," are attention, interpretation, judgment, and memory.
—Douglas T. Kenrick [127]

While the four core processes of thinking (attention, interpretations, judgments, and memory) remain the same for each person in regard to social cognition, the attributions or assumptions made by each person as a result of the process may very well be quite different. Like a vicious cycle, these differences in assumptions and conclusions stem from the differences in personal information which was originally gathered through this same process.[128]

As humans, we gather information from that which we choose to pay attention to. We then interpret that information through the unique personal experiences which we each have had— physically, emotionally, intellectually, and intuitively.

Judgment—the ever enticing "knowledge of good and evil"—then compels us to interpret and categorize our gathered information for memory storage. This newly acquired information, which may or may not be based on valid or sound logic, will then be used in the future to assist us again in the gathering of information and our subsequent decision making process.[129]

Stereotypes—Shortcutting the Process

Stereotypes are formulated because of expectations learned through previous experiences.[130] These expectations allow us to shortcut the entire thought processes of interpretation and judgment, relying on attention and memory to produce our conclusions and assumptions.[131]

While intended by nature to work for our benefit as a survival mechanism, the problem is that we as humans tend to pay more attention to our experiences when they support and confirm our expectations.[132] Subsequently, and creating the bypass which opens the door for error in our conclusions and assumptions, our thought process jumps from attention, and a subjectively chosen focus at that, straight to memory.[133] Little if any time is spent in reinterpreting the new information and, as a result, our assumptions and conclusions become based on previous experiences rather than on current, properly interpreted new information.[134] Our conclusions become biased, stereotyped, and literally pre-judged (i.e. prejudiced) and any errors in our conclusions become self-perpetuating.[135]

Critical Thinking

In 1945, mathematician George Polya (1887–1985) published a book titled *How to Solve It*, in which he demonstrated his approach to solving problems. His principles are as follows:

Polya's First Principle: Understand the Problem

To solve a problem, you have to understand the problem.

- Do you understand all the words used in stating the problem?

- What is the problem looking for?

- What data or information has been provided in the problem?

- Are there any special conditions mentioned in the problem that we need to consider in the solution?

- Can you restate the problem in your own words?

- Can you draw a picture or make a diagram that could help you solve the problem?

- Is there enough information in the problem to help you find a solution?

Polya's Second Principle: Devise a Plan

There are many different ways to solve a problem. The way you choose is based upon your own creativity, level of knowledge, and skills. Basically, solving the problem involves finding the connections that exist between the data you've been provided and the unknown you need to find.

- Have you seen or worked a problem similar to this before? Think about employing the strategies you used last time.

- Do you know related problems or concepts that would be helpful in finding the solution?

- Make a list of all the things you know and do not know.

- Look for a pattern in the problem.

- Draw a picture or diagram.

- Select the appropriate formula or concept.

- Use your creative thinking!

Polya's Third Principle: Carry Out the Plan

Once you've devised your plan, all you need to do is carry it through.

Be careful to follow all the steps necessary to get to the solution. Take time to reflect and check on each step as you work the problem.

Polya's Fourth Principle: Looking Back

Check your answer. Does it make sense?

Is it the solution that the problem was asking for?

Fallacies of Logic

Logic is based upon principles of reasoning and this reasoning takes on the form of either an argument or a *fallacy*.

An argument uses facts or assumption—called *premises*—to support a logical conclusion. On the other hand, a fallacy is a deceptive argument where the conclusion is not well supported by the premises.

We would like to think that fallacies are rare, but this would not be the case. The list below contains the most common fallacies of logic encountered:

Appeal to the Masses: This fallacy is based on the idea that since a lot of people believe something, then it must be true. Symbolically this can be represented as *many people believe that p is true, so therefore p is true*. Here's an example:

Premise: Most people believe the world is flat, Columbus....
Conclusion: Therefore, the world must be flat!

False Cause: This fallacy is based on the idea that a random action preceding an event is the cause of that event. Symbolically we can represent this fallacy as *because A came before B, then A caused B*. Example:

Premise: We kissed under the mistletoe,
Premise: Our baby was born nine months later,
Conclusion: Kissing will make you pregnant.

Appeal to Ignorance: This fallacy uses ignorance—a lack of knowledge—about the truth of a premise to conclude that the premise is false. Symbolically this can be represented as *since there is no proof that p is true, then p must be false.* Here's an example:

Premise: There is no evidence that Atlantis existed,
Conclusion: so, Atlantis never existed.

Hasty Generalization: In this fallacy, we reach a conclusion that two or more premises are the cause of a result without sufficient evidence to show that the premises are actually related. Symbolically, this can be stated as *if p and q are linked one or a few times, then p causes q*. Example:

Premise: I played the best game of my life yesterday,
Premise: Yesterday I was wearing this holey shirt,
Conclusion: Wearing this holey shirt caused me to play the best game of my life.

Limited Choice: This fallacy automatically assumes that the premise is false, so the opposite of the premise must be true without consideration of additional information. Symbolically, this can be represented as *since p is false, then only q (opposite of p) can be true.* Here's an example:

Premise: I do not support Lincoln's invasion of the South.
Conclusion: You must support the South's practice of slavery.

Appeal to Emotion: This fallacy appeals to emotions and completely avoids all logic. Symbolically, this can be represented as *p is associated with a strong positive emotion, therefore p is true.* Here is an example:

Premise: You love your kids
Conclusion: Then you must buy them this toy.

Abusive Ad Hominem: In this fallacy, the statement is considered false simply because of a prejudice against the person or group making the statement. Typically, this takes on the form of a personal attack with no basis in logic. Symbolically, this would be *since you disagree with the claim of p, then p is not true.* Example:

Premise: The marriage counselor has never been married.
Conclusion: His relationship advice can only end in disaster.

Circular Reasoning: This fallacy is simply an argument where the conclusion is just a rewording of the premise.

<u>Premise</u>: Our religious text is holy, and therefore inerrant.
<u>Conclusion</u>: Our religious text is inerrant because it is holy.

Diversion (*Red Herring*): In this fallacy, another problem is proposed to divert you from the real problem. In most cases, the two problems have little or no relation to one another.

<u>Premise</u>: We should not support the military due to the ethical questions of our military presence on foreign land.
<u>Conclusion</u>: Support for our military represents an ethical dilemma.

Straw Man: In this fallacy, a new argument is proposed that is a distorted version of the original argument. This new argument is meant to confuse and draw attention away from the real issue.

<u>Premise</u>: Legalized drugs would cut down on crime.
<u>Conclusion</u>: You must be using drugs.

CHAPTER NINE
Ritual, Culture and Social Identity

Without cultural sanction, most or all of our religious beliefs and rituals would fall into the domain of mental disturbance.

—John Schumacher[136]

Types of Rituals

Cultural rituals and ceremonies can typically be classified into three main categories: Seasonal Festivals (Yule, Ostara, Midsummer, etc.), Rites of Passage (marriage, parenthood, military service, etc.), and Initiatory and Religious Rites.

Seasonal Festivals

Joseph Campbell, in his book *The Power of Myth*, describes a ritual as,

.... the enactment of a myth. By participating in a ritual, you are participating in a myth.... In ancient times, that was the business of the teacher. He was to give you the clues to a spiritual life. That is what the priest was for. Also, that was what the ritual was for. A ritual can be defined as an enactment of a myth. By participating in a ritual, you are actually experiencing a mythological life. And it's out of that participation that one can learn to live spiritually."[137]

When we participate in seasonal rituals and ceremonies we are participating in the mythical life of the solar-hero, or -god. At Yule, for instance, we participate in the mythical birth of our Sun-god Balder. At Midsummer, as in the story of Balder who is mortally injured in the prime of his life, the Sun, reaching its own zenith of strength and vitality, begins to now descend towards its southern grave. From Midsummer to Yule we are reminded that all things, even the Sun-god Balder, must die. The hope and testimony of each seasonal cycle is thus found in the Sun's rebirth each Mother's Night, a promise of life, even after death.

Rites of Passage

Just as the seasonal ceremonies mark the journey and stages of the life of our Sun-god, rites of passage celebrate the participant's own passage through the stages of mortal life. In his 2010 book, *Child Development*, R. S. Feldman states that:

> Regardless of the nature of the ceremonies celebrated by various cultures, their underlying purpose tends to be similar from one culture to the next: symbolically celebrating the onset of the physical changes that turn a child's body into an adult body capable of reproduction. With these changes the child exits childhood and arrives at the doorstep of adulthood.[138]

66

Rites of passage also manifest the truth that with greater knowledge comes greater responsibilities. Subsequently, rites of passage not only celebrate the past accomplishments of the participant, but, accordingly also signify that greater responsibilities, duties, and obligations in relation to the social structure of the tribe have now been bestowed upon and have become the privilege of the participant.

Some typical rites of passage might include:

(Birth)

Puberty

Military

Marriage

Parenthood

Retirement

(Death)

In her article, *Ritual, Psychology, Carl Jung and Archetypes*, Kathryn Hughes writes,

> Sharing common rituals is a valuable uniting element for a culture. It helps unite the populace of a given community in their beliefs and values. The power of prayer and magick [sic] is generated through ritualistic practices. That power comes from the subconscious of those engaging in the ritual. The psychological aspects of ritual are tremendously important.[139]

Initiatory/Religious Rites

While rites of passage are typically naturally occurring or subsequent to the natural progression of one's mortal life, most often being something that happens upon the individual from his external environment, initiation and religious rites typically mark and align with one's directed interaction with their inner being and their resultant spiritual progression.

Like the organizational structure of academic institutions, one also finds a similar structure in regard to schools of spiritual instruction.

The most outer-order of religious or spiritual education is typically the exoteric, *for the masses,* type instruction offered by the local community priest. This instruction is primarily focused on creating a minimum level of spiritual knowledge and "competence" within and among the priests' society.

The real beginning of one's esoteric, or *for the few,* type training begins in undergraduate school where, rather than dogmatic instruction pigeon holed by sectarian agenda, one begins to see the academic and historical history and theological development of their childhood religion in all of its true, realistic, and at times not so pretty glory.

Should one desire more spiritual training they then pass on into graduate school and ministerial seminary. Now, having learned to study all religions with the same "critical" eye, the student is free to uninhibitedly investigate any and all religious beliefs and systems to further understand their own.

Finally, an aspirant may come to the doors of a Mystery School of any number of traditions. These schools are intended for initiatory training in one's ultimate return to The Source of All Knowledge and Consciousness, The Self.

Whether initiated as a member of the local religious organization or a mystical order, the ultimate purpose is always to see to it that….

> …. all initiates are ethically trained in order to become balanced, productive and most importantly conscious members of the lodge and of society as a whole. In Masonic terms, the new initiate is compared to a rough-hewn stone which is to be finished by the mason.[140]

Identity Formation Dilemma

Although the path to forming an identity is often difficult enough for adolescents, it presents a particular challenge for our children in 21st century America.

On the one hand, adolescents are told that society should be color-blind, that race and ethnic background should not matter in terms of opportunities and achievement. Based on a traditional *cultural assimilation model,* this view holds that individual cultural identities should be assimilated into a unified culture in the United States—the proverbial melting pot model.

On the other hand, the *pluralistic society model* suggests that U.S. society is made up of diverse, coequal cultural groups that should preserve their individual cultural features. The pluralistic society model grew in part from the belief that the cultural assimilation model denigrates one's cultural heritage and lowers children's self-esteem.

From this perspective, identity development includes development of racial and ethnic identity—the sense of membership in a racial or ethnic group and the feelings that are associated with that membership.

Intrinsic to the pluralistic society model as well is that it fosters a personal and inherent sense of commitment, responsibility, and duty to one's particular racial or ethnic group, nurturing again one's sense of inclusion and belonging within that community.[141]

CHAPTER TEN
Gnostic Initiation

Behind the veil of all the hieratic and mystical allegories of ancient doctrines, behind the darkness and strange ordeals of all initiations, under the seal of all sacred writings, in the ruins of Nineveh or Thebes, on the crumbling stones of old temples and on the blackened visage of the Assyrian or Egyptian sphinx, in the monstrous or marvelous paintings which interpret to the faithful of India the inspired pages of the Vedas, in the cryptic emblems of our old books on alchemy, in the ceremonies practiced at reception by all secret societies, there are found indications of a doctrine which is everywhere the same and everywhere carefully concealed.

—Eliphas Levi[142]

The structure and intent of ancient gnostic initiatory rites, as with initiatory rites of today, is to instruct the participant in the development of divine attributes and noble virtues. The curriculum of instruction and training would vary depending on the discipline under consideration; however, the outline and format of these systems were modeled after nature and so tend to remain constant even among seemingly opposed systems.

As a result of their observations of nature and its ordered design, the ancients would typically associate the four classical elements (air, fire, water, and earth) with various levels of conscious awareness, and the seven visible planets of antiquity (Saturn, Jupiter, Mars, Sol, Venus, Mercury, and Luna), with each of their corresponding ancient virtues.[143]

Elemental Model

The gnostic initiatory rites were meant to represent the progression toward deification and awakening, and they held that it was the four classical elements of antiquity that represented the various stages of conscious illumination. Progression from one stage to the other was marked by passing through an initiatory ritual celebrated between each of the four elemental stages.

Considering this initiatory structure, we find that earth represents the consciousness obsessed with the mortal passions and enslaved by matter on one extreme, and fire representing the conscious awakening of the initiate on the other extreme. Accordingly:

> ⚜ The practitioner who developed a mastery over their emotions would be eligible to receive the initiation associated with water;

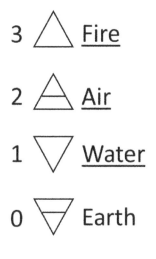

❧ The practitioner who developed a mastery over their intellect would be eligible to receive the initiation associated with air; and,

❧ The practitioner who developed a mastery in spiritual understanding and metaphysical law would be eligible to receive the initiation associated with fire.

Earth to Water

The initial level of consciousness attributed to the seeker at this stage of instruction is represented by the element earth and corresponds to a conscious level which is totally obsessed with the physical world and one's own ego. Symbolically this is often represented by the inverted pentagram—depicting the four

elements (the four arms of the star) above and in control of the "self" or "spirit." This first stage of Gnostic initiation then is generally concerned with subduing the passions and the development of noble virtues.

The purpose of this stage of instruction, meditation, and ritual practice is to give the initiate those experiences which will reveal that we as humans do not exist as mere physical beings; but, that we also exist as pure consciousness, or spirit, as well. This is the stage in which the initiate consciously realizes the physical illusion of this world.

Water to Air

The next gnostic initiation is associated with air or breath and is called "pneumatic". Since the Divine was understood as One with creation, then the pneumatic initiate in the gnostic schools would undertake studies in the arts and sciences to better understand, glorify, and imitate those Holy Powers. A pneumatic initiate came to realize their nature in objective terms and the Divine Nature as being emanating and inclusive as the "One". Duality in nature is seen from a more transcended perspective and all experiences and relationships begin to be brought into Oneness with Divinity. The initiate and the Divine become united as "The Mystery" in adoration of itself.

Air to Fire

The last phase of gnostic initiatory training is usually symbolic of and corresponding to a "baptism by fire." An initiate is expected to have by now transcended the concept of Duality through study, meditation, and practice. There is also a very real, very authentic and sensational death of the initiate's old lower, profane and surface-thinking self, accompanied by a recognizable and distinct resurrection (i.e. "awakening") of a new "spiritually minded" self. It is this "Higher-self" that is now "redeemed" and liberated to be expressed by the new adept as a perfect reproduction and reflection of the Holy Powers present at the center of human consciousness. Symbolic of this stage of initiation is the upright pentagram, depicting now the spiritual Self above and no longer being controlled by, but in control of the physical, elemental forces of nature.

Planetary Model

It was during the Pneumatic stage of initiation, from the conscious level of "water to air," when most schools of gnostic philosophy associated their initiatory training with the seven visual planets of antiquity. The mystical Pythagoreans and other occult schools also associated these seven initiatory steps with the seven noble metals; the seven days of the week; the seven liberal arts and sciences; the notes of the musical octave; the seven colors of light; and, the seven traditional vowels. Contemporary Teutonic philosopher Jacob Boehme would often refer to these as the Seven Qualities.[144]

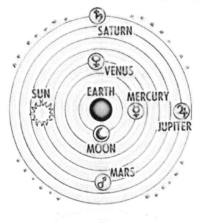

It is held in gnostic philosophy that as souls incarnate down to earth from the highest heavens they pass through all the planetary spheres and assimilate those tools of consciousness needed for incarnation. As these souls incarnate they also take on the vices and virtues of these planetary influences.

After death, or as a result of enlightenment experienced within initiatory exercises and rituals, the soul ascends back to the higher realms of consciousness by the same planetary path. This is the path for returning to pure Gnosis.

CHAPTER ELEVEN
An Esoteric Norse Tradition

In a warrior's league...the rites of initiation ought to be generally the same. They have in common an initiation through symbolic death and hence they are living deads.

—Ingemar Nordgren[145]

The Myth

In Norse mythology, the Einherjar are Odin's chosen warriors who have either died in battle or through an initiatory death in devoted service to Him.[146] After their death—be it physical or symbolic—the Einherjar then "dwell" with Odin in one of the twelve halls of Asgard called Valhalla, the great *hall of the slain*. There in Valhalla the Einherjar practice and hone their combat skills in preparation for Ragnarok, the final conflict between the Asgardian/Einherjar alliance and the forces of chaos.[147]

Until Ragnarok—the commencement of which is marked by an attack on Bifrost,[148] the sounding of Heimdall's Gjallarhorn,[149] and the mustering of all who would protect both Asgard and the Norse World Tree, Yggdrasill—the Einherjar pass eternity away in Odin's graces by battle training during the day[150] and then feasting on mead and pork with Him in Valhalla each night.[151]

Of Odin's great hall Valhalla itself it is said that eight-hundred Einherjar can pass through each one of its five-hundred and forty doors at a single time.[152] We are also told that Valhalla's roof is made from the warrior's shields and that the hall's pillars are constructed from their battle spears.[153]

The Ordeal

The way of the Einherjar and journey to Valhalla's doors, as one would expect of a warrior's path, is seeded with many natural barriers, wild beasts, and magical spells—ordeals specifically designed and strategically placed to test the fortitude and resolve of the approaching knight.[154] Joseph Campbell, one of the twentieth century's leading comparative mythologists, describes the intents of these "trials" as being:

> designed to see to it that the intending hero should be really a hero. Is he really a match for this task? Can he overcome the dangers? Does he have the courage, the knowledge, the capacity, *to enable him to serve*? (emphasis added)[155]

In her book, *The Masks of Odin: Wisdom of the Ancient Norse,* Elsa-Brita Titchenell gives us a brief idea of this ancient shamanistic path.[156] Einherjar, she points out, must overcome the wolfhounds named Gere and Freke, "greed" and "gluttony," and master the rivers of "time" and "doubt" without being devoured by their innate animal nature. It is, as Titchenell tells us, through these and other trials along the path to Valhalla's gates that:

> the higher self or spirit of man permits the human ego to be tested in the fires of the soul to prove its integrity. If successful, the man brings to birth his inner god, the mortal earns its immortality, uniting with the indwelling divinity.[157]

The Model

Scholars suggest that the model for the Einherjar myth is a first century sect of Odin worshipers. These mortal Einherjar consisted of many Scandinavian kings, princes, and warriors.[158] It is from stanza 60 of the Norse tale *Lokasenna*—where we read of Loki calling Thor an *Einheri*, the singular of Einherjar—that linguistic scholars link the Einherjar myth and its origins with the Harii people, the first century tribe mentioned by Tacitus as an "army of the dead."[159]

The "army of the dead" motif can be traced back to the Proto-Indo-European Aryan fertility god Indra of the Vedic period

(2000 – 500 BCE). Indra here is portrayed as leader of the Maruts—which was considered an army of dead charged with scaring demons from the farmlands to promote fertility and a good harvest in the future months.[160] The development of this army of dead souls continued through the death-god Rudra,[161] who replaced Indra, on through to the Mysteries of Hermes in Greece as well as the Roman halls of Mercurius.[162]

Ingemar Nordgren, in his book *The Well Spring of the Goths,* emphasizes that the myths and legends of Valhalla, the Einherjar, and Ragnarok should also be considered and understood "within the frames of a warrior's league of secret character,"[163] and that Odin's warriors, with the Hadjings under the command of Freya, ought to be viewed as being "shamanistic" in nature when interpreting their historical and mythical accounts.[164]

The Question

Interpreted in such a fashion, what should be said of Bifrost, that bridge connecting humanity with Asgard?[165] How should we view the image of Heimdall—guardian of that bridge?[166] And, how might one interpret the myth of Ragnarok and the threat upon Bifrost as an Einherjar—an initiate in Odin's secret gnostic warrior league?

CHAPTER TWELVE
Gnostic Thought in North Mythology

We have allowed some truths of our faith to be occluded as other people try to adorn it with their own ideas or opinions or hypotheses until it becomes stirred up and stirred up and we have to get back to where we began.

—Bryan Wilton[167]

Like most world religions, Asatru would not typically be categorized as an Esoteric or Gnostic religion, per se; but, like so many of the world's religions, Asatru's religious texts contain numerous mystical, esoteric, and shamanistic elements rooted in gnostic philosophy and a metaphysical worldview.[168] Subsequently, it would follow that the myths of Asatru are best understood and interpreted by relating them to gnostic philosophy as allegorical tales meant to lead us to gnosis.

Odin's "Self" Sacrifice

Of the world's sixteen most notable crucified deities,[169] perhaps the most obvious depiction of this event as an intended and symbolized shamanistic and initiatory act rather than an actual ceasing of the participant's mortal life is that of Odin's sacrifice of himself to his Self.[170] Collin Cleary, in his article *What God Did Odin Worship*, writes:

> What is given in the Edda, it bears remembering, is a myth. It is not a report of an actual event. It is a mythic description of a magical act of initiation. One of the central tenets of Edred Thorsson's Odinism is the claim that Odin is an exemplar of the Left Hand Path – the path precisely of Evola's Kundalini/Alchemy (or Raja Yoga/Royal Art). One does not "worship" Odin, one identifies with him. What is described in the Edda is a path of initiation we ourselves may follow, into the runic mysteries. It is a path of asceticism, and of self-overcoming, in which we awaken within us a dormant power than can confer knowledge of mysteries.[171]

While there is well documented evidence that the ancient indigenous European peoples maintained a priest class for teaching and guiding their tribes in interpreting the lore, propagating the traditions, and dispensing discipline, these priests were never raised to a position of arbiter or mediator between the practitioner and the Holy Powers.[172] The personal study and acquisition of knowledge pertaining to the natural sciences, human psychology and the cosmic spheres by each initiate were intended to reveal the secrets of nature and the occult character of the Divine to the participant—this is the "gnosis" which would lead to one's realization of their own divine nature, a "gnosis" which cannot be taught but must be individually experienced.[173]

During my studies in Sufi dharma I was intrigued by the practice of the giving and receiving of the turban. The turban is seen as one's spiritual "crown" and it is given in the ceremony by the "seeker," the self, to the newly initiated "neophyte," the newly awakened or realized Self—both being the one and the same individual. Essentially, you give yourself your spiritual crown, a very powerful symbol when realized internally and on a spiritual and even psychological level.

It is the aim of ancient gnostic instruction to lead us, in Norse vernacular, to the discovery that we are each united by Odin revealing Himself—in word, thought, and deed—through our individual and distinct "selves." Duality is not abolished, but understood and defined through unity and harmony.

Bifrost—Mystical Bridge to the Gods

In his multivolume work, *Teutonic Mythology: Gods and Goddesses of the Northland*, Viktor Rydberg, concluding his examination of Gylfaginning's cosmographical and eschatological designs regarding Bifrost and Yggdrasil, referred to Gylfaginning's model as "a monstrous caricature of the mythology, a caricature which is continued….in a confused and contradictory manner."[174]

While there is always believed to be some degree of historical truth in the events surrounding many of the myths, no matter which culture they generate from, it cannot be emphasized enough that spiritual literature (i.e. myths) needs to be interpreted as spiritual literature and not literal, historic, or scientific records. To do so to any culture's mythological tales is to invite nothing but a perverted and grotesque rendering of the intended mystical message.

In comparison with and contrast to all such good intentioned yet "confused and contradictory" attempts at a plausible and applicable rendering of the Bifrost myth, there is of course always the simplest interpretation drawn straight from the myth, ironically, practically literally: Bifrost is that very fragile bridge to the gods consisting of three colors, each representing one of the three elements.

Taken "spiritually," Bifrost can be seen as simply that which connects us with the Aesir—be it a tradition, a custom, a ritual, etc. Detailed within the myths as having three colors (considered representational of the elements), we can also see the bridge being constructed of the three tiered levels of conscious awareness used as a gnostic "literary symbol" of mankind's progressive illumination toward the realms of the gods and their own deification. Interpreting the myths in such a fashion neither violates associated "lore" nor contradicts any known symbolic meanings. Actually, given the historical, textural, and archeological evidences regarding ancient religious beliefs and symbols used to express such messages, there is more than sufficient support for a metaphysical interpretation of Bifrost along these lines.

Heimdall—Guardian of Bifrost

When considering the myth of Heimdall, perhaps the most significant indication that a mystical interpretation of his identity, office and function is in order is that he is said to have "seven" mothers. As this is a physical impossibility it should amount to, and is intended to be, a literary slap-in-the-face to get you to stop and examine the storyline more closely.

Merging the esoteric interpretations of Bifrost with that of its guardian, Heimdall (the runes (secrets) are tattooed on his lip/tongue, he can see with the sight of an eagle, and he can hear the grass grow), we begin to see Heimdall as an archetypal Guardian of the Norse Tradition.

Complimenting the idea of Heimdall as the archetypal inspector/guardian of the Norse tradition is his role as Rig. In the *Song of Rig*, Heimdall travels through Midgard disguised as the king Rig and fathers the progenitors of what some consider the three classes of Norse society or even the three races of humanity.

Considering the *Song of Rig* in light of other myths and known initiatory systems of instruction that describe humanity's progressive ascent back to the Source of consciousness, we can readily see that the three-tiered structure Rig fathered represents more than mere social classes or root races, but a progressive assent, once again, of humanity's conscious awareness.

Pythagoras, for instance, described similar progressive stages in the tale of three types of men who attend a fair. The first is a merchant who sees a chance for profit and is associated with the first level of consciousness and the lower three "soul-centers". The second man is the hero attending the fair to compete in its games and to win glory. This second man is influenced by the soul-center of the heart and is associated with the second level of conscious awareness. Pythagoras then calls the third man a philosopher, who comes to the fair to simply observe and contemplate. The philosopher, according to Pythagoras, is influenced by the upper three soul-centers and is associated with the third and highest level of conscious awareness.[175]

Plato also described this pattern of development towards the perfect society in his work, *The Republic*. To become a "citizen" in his utopia one develops certain virtues through particular studies along a progressive path toward developing the noble character of the community leader, the philosopher-king. The three stages of growth in Plato's society are the worker, the warrior, and the philosopher.

Understood in light of ancient patterns laid out to serve as "literary symbols," Heimdall takes on this additional layer of esoteric significance. Having already considered Heimdall as an archetype of the guardian of Norse tradition, we see now through the Song of Rig that he might very well represent the father of the Norse initiatory system and archetype of every Norse Initiate also as a Guardian of the Norse tradition, born of the seven "mothers" that nurture the aspirant along the seven progressive stages of character development; and, an active participant in the progressive initiatory training of "wanderer," "warrior," and "wizard" within the Northern Mysteries.

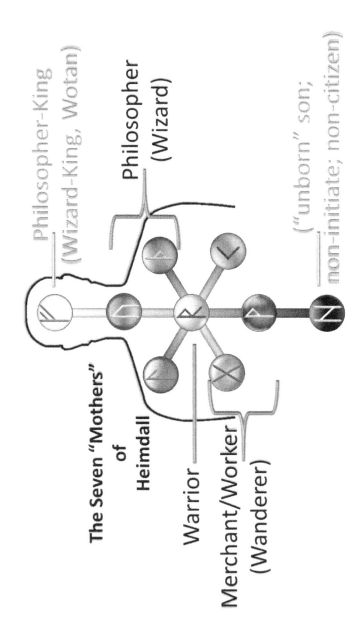

CHAPTER THIRTEEN
Applied Psychology for Today's Asatruar

There is a group that may not have acquired the true spirit....or the ideals of the spirituality which we hold so dear....our obligation is to step up to a higher game and higher level of play and a higher demonstration of understanding of these things that we are about[; and,] in stepping up to the plate and demonstrating higher ideals of spirituality in what is the original idea of Asatru in the United States, we will have the opportunity to escape the errors and miseries [of today's sectarian strife].

—Bryan Wilton[176]

Among Asatru Folk there is a set of character traits which encapsulates those noble virtues expressed most often by our gods and heroes. Adapting both ancient initiatory techniques and Benjamin Franklin's techniques for becoming a virtuous man,[177] a similar nine-week exercise can be specifically tailored for training in and assimilation of the Odinist/Asatru Folk Nine Noble Virtues.[178]

Each week, in conjunction with the regular observance of each of the virtues throughout the day, a specific virtue is also emphasized. A black dot is used in the appropriate column of the tracking records provided for failure to express a virtue; and, an empty or white dot is used to indicate that the virtue was expressed (a gray or numeric scale may also be used to indicated degrees of expression). At the end of the day the tracking record is reviewed and commented on for further and future reference.

Similar templates are used in the Process of Thinking, Leadership Traits Development and Living the Runes journaling exercises as well. The Process of Thinking exercise is a four-week personal assessment on one's ability to manifest thoughts and ideas into reality through the process of critical thinking. The Leadership Traits Development exercise is modeled around the fourteen U. S. Marine Corps Leadership Traits. Living the Runes is an exercise which focuses on one of the twenty-four runes of the Elder Futhark each week, amounting to a full twenty-four-week (six month) preparatory exercise for further studies in advanced operative runology.

Concluding these consecutive fifty-one weeks of self-analysis, self-evaluation, and self-assessment, the final week of the year's curriculum is dedicated to, you guessed it, a journaling exercise regarding one's growth, maturity and working knowledge of each of the primary areas investigated—critical thinking, character improvement, small-group leadership, and operative runology.

The psychology behind these exercises is found in the phenomena of our lives changing almost the instant we begin to pay attention to it. By focusing our attention on these skills, virtues, traits, and cultural images they will begin to express themselves more and more in our lives. Eventually, when we can subconsciously express the influences of these etheric concepts and ideas through our character, behavior, attitudes, and mannerisms on a daily basis, we will have begun to acquire the nature of the gods.

WAY OF THE EINHERJAR I

PRACTICAL APPLICATION EXERCISES

The operative runologist must first and foremost be dedicated to the development of the self—of the very capacity or ability to do magic. This development consists of three components, the internalization of three things: staves, myths, and culture. The meanings and very living essence of each of the rune staves must be absorbed into one's very being. The myths must likewise be synthesized into one's being. Finally, the general underlying cultural principles which eternally give shape to our mysteries must be understood and absorbed. This is a process which requires time and considerable effort. But without it operative runology is difficult to effect.

—Edred Thorsson[179]

RESEARCH ~ CONTEMPLATE ~ APPLY ~ RECORD

The Process of Thinking (4 weeks)

Nine Virtues Character Builder (9 weeks)

Leadership Traits Development (14 weeks)

Living the Runes (24 weeks)

Cumulative Assessment (1 week)

The Process of Thinking

Four-Week Journaling Exercise #1

Einherjar—Gnostic Warriors of the North

WEEK ONE TRACKER: ATTENTION

Inspirational Quote on Attention:

Initial concept or idea of Attention:

Initial thoughts on Attention to Detail skills:

Attention							
	M	**T**	**W**	**TH**	**F**	**S**	**S**
Attention							
Interpretation							
Judgement							
Memory							

WEEK ONE NOTES—The Process of Thinking

Concluding concepts or ideas on Attention:

Concluding thoughts on Attention to Detail skills:

WEEK TWO TRACKER: INTERPRETATION

Inspirational Quote on Interpretation:

Initial concept or idea of Interpretation:

Initial thoughts on Interpretation and Comprehension skills:

Interpretation							
	M	**T**	**W**	**TH**	**F**	**S**	**S**
Attention							
Interpretation							
Judgement							
Memory							

WEEK TWO NOTES—The Process of Thinking

Concluding concepts or ideas on Interpretation

Initial thoughts on Interpretation and Comprehension skills:

WEEK THREE TRACKER: JUDGEMENT

Inspirational Quote on Judgement:

Initial concept or idea of Judgement:

Initial thoughts on Judgement and fallacies of logic:

Judgement							
	M	**T**	**W**	**TH**	**F**	**S**	**S**
Attention							
Interpretation							
Judgement							
Memory							

WEEK THREE NOTES—The Process of Thinking

Concluding concepts or ideas on Judgement:

Concluding thoughts on Judgement and fallacies of logic:

WEEK FOUR TRACKER: MEMORY

Inspirational Quote on Memory:

Initial concept or idea of Memory:

Initial thoughts on Memory skills:

Memory							
	M	**T**	**W**	**TH**	**F**	**S**	**S**
Attention							
Interpretation							
Judgement							
Memory							

WEEK FOUR NOTES—The Process of Thinking

Concluding concepts or ideas on Memory:

Concluding thoughts on Memory skills:

The Process of Thinking
Four-Week Analysis of the Exercise

Process of Thinking Analysis of the Exercise

The Nine Virtues Character Builder

Nine-Week Journaling Exercise #2

WEEK ONE TRACKER: COURAGE

Inspirational Quote on Courage:

Initial concept or idea of Courage:

Courage							
	M	**T**	**W**	**TH**	**F**	**S**	**S**
Courage							
Truth							
Honor							
Fidelity							
Discipline							
Hospitality							
Industriousness							
Self-reliance							
Perseverance							

WEEK ONE NOTES—Nine Virtues Character Builder

Definition:

Etymology:

Concluding concepts or ideas on Courage:

WEEK TWO TRACKER: TRUTH

Inspirational Quote on Truth:

Initial concept or idea of Truth:

Truth							
	M	**T**	**W**	**TH**	**F**	**S**	**S**
Courage							
Truth							
Honor							
Fidelity							
Discipline							
Hospitality							
Industriousness							
Self-reliance							
Perseverance							

WEEK TWO NOTES—Nine Virtues Character Builder

Definition:

Etymology:

Concluding concepts or ideas on Truth:

WEEK THREE TRACKER: HONOR

Inspirational Quote on Honor:

Initial concept or idea of Honor:

Honor							
	M	**T**	**W**	**TH**	**F**	**S**	**S**
Courage							
Truth							
Honor							
Fidelity							
Discipline							
Hospitality							
Industriousness							
Self-reliance							
Perseverance							

WEEK THREE NOTES—Nine Virtues Character Builder

Definition:

Etymology:

Concluding concepts or ideas on Honor:

WEEK FOUR TRACKER: FIDELITY

Inspirational Quote on Fidelity:

Initial concept or idea of Fidelity:

Fidelity							
	M	**T**	**W**	**TH**	**F**	**S**	**S**
Courage							
Truth							
Honor							
Fidelity							
Discipline							
Hospitality							
Industriousness							
Self-reliance							
Perseverance							

WEEK FOUR NOTES—Nine Virtues Character Builder

Definition:

Etymology:

Concluding concepts or ideas on Fidelity:

WEEK FIVE TRACKER: DISCIPLINE

Inspirational Quote on Discipline:

Initial concept or idea of Discipline:

Discipline							
	M	T	W	TH	F	S	S
Courage							
Truth							
Honor							
Fidelity							
Discipline							
Hospitality							
Industriousness							
Self-reliance							
Perseverance							

WEEK FIVE NOTES—Nine Virtues Character Builder

Definition:

Etymology:

Concluding concepts or ideas on Discipline:

WEEK SIX TRACKER: HOSPITALITY

Inspirational Quote on Hospitality:

Initial concept or idea of Hospitality:

Hospitality							
	M	**T**	**W**	**TH**	**F**	**S**	**S**
Courage							
Truth							
Honor							
Fidelity							
Discipline							
Hospitality							
Industriousness							
Self-reliance							
Perseverance							

WEEK SIX NOTES—Nine Virtues Character Builder

Definition:

Etymology:

Concluding concepts or ideas on Hospitality:

WEEK SEVEN TRACKER: INDUSTRIOUSNESS

Inspirational Quote on Industriousness:

Initial concept or idea of Industriousness:

Industriousness							
	M	**T**	**W**	**TH**	**F**	**S**	**S**
Courage							
Truth							
Honor							
Fidelity							
Discipline							
Hospitality							
Industriousness							
Self-reliance							
Perseverance							

WEEK SEVEN NOTES—Nine Virtues Character Builder

Definition:

Etymology:

Concluding concepts or ideas on Industriousness:

WEEK EIGHT TRACKER: SELF-RELIANCE

Inspirational Quote on Self-reliance:

Initial concept or idea of Self-reliance:

Self-reliance							
	M	T	W	TH	F	S	S
Courage							
Truth							
Honor							
Fidelity							
Discipline							
Hospitality							
Industriousness							
Self-reliance							
Perseverance							

WEEK EIGHT NOTES—Nine Virtues Character Builder

Definition:

Etymology:

Concluding concepts or ideas on Self-reliance:

WEEK NINE TRACKER: PERSEVERANCE

Inspirational Quote on Perseverance:

Initial concept or idea of Perseverance:

Perseverance							
	M	**T**	**W**	**TH**	**F**	**S**	**S**
Courage							
Truth							
Honor							
Fidelity							
Discipline							
Hospitality							
Industriousness							
Self-reliance							
Perseverance							

WEEK NINE NOTES—Nine Virtues Character Builder

Definition:

Etymology:

Concluding concepts or ideas on Perseverance:

The Nine Noble Virtues Character Builder
Nine-Week Analysis of the Exercise

Character Builder Analysis of the Exercise

Leadership Traits Development

Fourteen-Week Journaling Exercise #3

WEEK ONE TRACKER: JUSTICE

Inspirational Quote on Justice:

Justice							
	M	T	W	TH	F	S	S
Justice							
Judgement							
Dependability							
Initiative							
Decisiveness							
Tact							
Integrity							
Enthusiasm							
Bearing							
Unselfishness							
Courage							
Knowledge							
Loyalty							
Endurance							

WEEK ONE NOTES—Leadership Traits Development

Definition of Justice:

Etymology of the word Justice:

How can this be applied in regard to being a leader?

WEEK TWO TRACKER: JUDGEMENT

Inspirational Quote on Judgement:

Judgement							
	M	**T**	**W**	**TH**	**F**	**S**	**S**
Justice							
Judgement							
Dependability							
Initiative							
Decisiveness							
Tact							
Integrity							
Enthusiasm							
Bearing							
Unselfishness							
Courage							
Knowledge							
Loyalty							
Endurance							

WEEK TWO NOTES—Leadership Traits Development

Definition of Judgement:

Etymology of the word Judgement:

How can this be applied in regard to being a leader?

WEEK THREE TRACKER: DEPENDABILITY

Inspirational Quote on Dependability:

Dependability							
	M	T	W	TH	F	S	S
Justice							
Judgement							
Dependability							
Initiative							
Decisiveness							
Tact							
Integrity							
Enthusiasm							
Bearing							
Unselfishness							
Courage							
Knowledge							
Loyalty							
Endurance							

WEEK THREE NOTES—Leadership Traits Development

Definition of Dependability:

Etymology of the word Dependability:

How can this be applied in regard to being a leader?

WEEK FOUR TRACKER: INITIATIVE

Inspirational Quote on Initiative:

Initiative							
	M	T	W	TH	F	S	S
Justice							
Judgement							
Dependability							
Initiative							
Decisiveness							
Tact							
Integrity							
Enthusiasm							
Bearing							
Unselfishness							
Courage							
Knowledge							
Loyalty							
Endurance							

WEEK FOUR NOTES—Leadership Traits Development

Definition of Initiative:

Etymology of the word Initiative:

How can this be applied in regard to being a leader?

WEEK FIVE TRACKER: DECISIVENESS

Inspirational Quote on Decisiveness:

Decisiveness							
	M	T	W	TH	F	S	S
Justice							
Judgement							
Dependability							
Initiative							
Decisiveness							
Tact							
Integrity							
Enthusiasm							
Bearing							
Unselfishness							
Courage							
Knowledge							
Loyalty							
Endurance							

WEEK FIVE NOTES—Leadership Traits Development

Definition of Decisiveness:

Etymology of the word Decisiveness:

How can this be applied in regard to being a leader?

WEEK SIX TRACKER: TACT

Inspirational Quote on Tact:

Tact							
	M	**T**	**W**	**TH**	**F**	**S**	**S**
Justice							
Judgement							
Dependability							
Initiative							
Decisiveness							
Tact							
Integrity							
Enthusiasm							
Bearing							
Unselfishness							
Courage							
Knowledge							
Loyalty							
Endurance							

WEEK SIX NOTES—Leadership Traits Development

Definition of Tact:

Etymology of the word Tact:

How can this be applied in regard to being a leader?

WEEK SEVEN TRACKER: INTEGRITY

Inspirational Quote on Integrity:

Integrity							
	M	T	W	TH	F	S	S
Justice							
Judgement							
Dependability							
Initiative							
Decisiveness							
Tact							
Integrity							
Enthusiasm							
Bearing							
Unselfishness							
Courage							
Knowledge							
Loyalty							
Endurance							

WEEK SEVEN NOTES—Leadership Traits Development

Definition of Integrity:

Etymology of the word Integrity:

How can this be applied in regard to being a leader?

WEEK EIGHT TRACKER: ENTHUSIASM

Inspirational Quote on Enthusiasm:

Enthusiasm							
	M	T	W	TH	F	S	S
Justice							
Judgement							
Dependability							
Initiative							
Decisiveness							
Tact							
Integrity							
Enthusiasm							
Bearing							
Unselfishness							
Courage							
Knowledge							
Loyalty							
Endurance							

WEEK EIGHT NOTES—Leadership Traits Development

Definition of Enthusiasm:

Etymology of the word Enthusiasm:

How can this be applied in regard to being a leader?

WEEK NINE TRACKER: BEARING

Inspirational Quote on Bearing:

Bearing							
	M	T	W	TH	F	S	S
Justice							
Judgement							
Dependability							
Initiative							
Decisiveness							
Tact							
Integrity							
Enthusiasm							
Bearing							
Unselfishness							
Courage							
Knowledge							
Loyalty							
Endurance							

WEEK NINE NOTES—Leadership Traits Development

Definition of Bearing:

Etymology of the word Bearing:

How can this be applied in regard to being a leader?

WEEK TEN TRACKER: UNSELFISHNESS

Inspirational Quote on Unselfishness:

Unselfishness							
	M	T	W	TH	F	S	S
Justice							
Judgement							
Dependability							
Initiative							
Decisiveness							
Tact							
Integrity							
Enthusiasm							
Bearing							
Unselfishness							
Courage							
Knowledge							
Loyalty							
Endurance							

WEEK TEN NOTES—Leadership Traits Development

Definition of Unselfishness:

Etymology of the word Unselfishness:

How can this be applied in regard to being a leader?

WEEK ELEVEN TRACKER: COURAGE

Inspirational Quote on Courage:

Courage							
	M	**T**	**W**	**TH**	**F**	**S**	**S**
Justice							
Judgement							
Dependability							
Initiative							
Decisiveness							
Tact							
Integrity							
Enthusiasm							
Bearing							
Unselfishness							
Courage							
Knowledge							
Loyalty							
Endurance							

WEEK ELEVEN NOTES—Leadership Traits Development

Definition of Courage:

Etymology of the word Courage:

How can this be applied in regard to being a leader?

WEEK TWELVE TRACKER: KNOWLEDGE

Inspirational Quote on Knowledge:

Knowledge							
	M	**T**	**W**	**TH**	**F**	**S**	**S**
Justice							
Judgement							
Dependability							
Initiative							
Decisiveness							
Tact							
Integrity							
Enthusiasm							
Bearing							
Unselfishness							
Courage							
Knowledge							
Loyalty							
Endurance							

WEEK TWELVE NOTES—Leadership Traits Development

Definition of Knowledge:

Etymology of the word Knowledge:

How can this be applied in regard to being a leader?

WEEK THIRTEEN TRACKER: LOYALTY

Inspirational Quote on Loyalty:

Loyalty							
	M	T	W	TH	F	S	S
Justice							
Judgement							
Dependability							
Initiative							
Decisiveness							
Tact							
Integrity							
Enthusiasm							
Bearing							
Unselfishness							
Courage							
Knowledge							
Loyalty							
Endurance							

WEEK THIRTEEN NOTES—Leadership Traits Development

Definition of Loyalty:

Etymology of the word Loyalty:

How can this be applied in regard to being a leader?

WEEK FOURTEEN TRACKER: ENDURANCE

Inspirational Quote on Endurance:

Endurance							
	M	T	W	TH	F	S	S
Justice							
Judgement							
Dependability							
Initiative							
Decisiveness							
Tact							
Integrity							
Enthusiasm							
Bearing							
Unselfishness							
Courage							
Knowledge							
Loyalty							
Endurance							

WEEK FOURTEEN NOTES—Leadership Traits Development

Definition of Endurance:

Etymology of the word Endurance:

How can this be applied in regard to being a leader?

Leadership Traits Development
Fourteen-Week Analysis of the Exercise

Leadership Traits Development Analysis of the Exercise

Living the Runes

Twenty-four-Week Journaling Exercise #4

Einherjar—Gnostic Warriors of the North

WEEK ONE TRACKER: FEHU ᚠ, f

MOBLE PROPERTY, CATTLE

Inspirational Quote on Fehu:

Initial concept or idea of Fehu:

Ætt One; Fehu ᚠ							
	M	**T**	**W**	**TH**	**F**	**S**	**S**
Fehu (ᚠ)							
Uruz (ᚢ)							
THurisaz (ᚦ)							
Ansuz (ᚨ)							
Raidho (ᚱ)							
Kenaz (ᚲ)							
Gebo (ᚷ)							
Wunjo (ᚹ)							

WEEK ONE NOTES—Living the Runes
Key words:

Personal experiences/gleanings of Fehu's influence:

Concluding concepts or ideas on Fehu:

WEEK TWO TRACKER: URUZ ᚢ, u, v

THE AUROCHS

Inspirational Quote on Uruz:

Initial concept or idea of Uruz:

Ætt One; Uruz ᚢ							
	M	**T**	**W**	**TH**	**F**	**S**	**S**
Fehu (ᚠ)							
Uruz (ᚢ)							
THurisaz (ᚦ)							
Ansuz (ᚨ)							
Raidho (ᚱ)							
Kenaz (ᚲ)							
Gebo (ᚷ)							
Wunjo (ᚹ)							

WEEK TWO NOTES—Living the Runes
Key words:

Personal experiences/gleanings of Uruz's influence:

Concluding concepts or ideas on Uruz:

WEEK THREE TRACKER: THURISAZ Þ, th

THE STRONG ONE

Inspirational Quote on Thurisaz:

Initial concept or idea of Thurisaz:

Ætt One; Thurisaz Þ							
	M	T	W	TH	F	S	S
Fehu (ᚠ)							
Uruz (ᚢ)							
THurisaz (Þ)							
Ansuz (ᚨ)							
Raidho (ᚱ)							
Kenaz (ᚲ)							
Gebo (ᚷ)							
Wunjo (ᚹ)							

WEEK THREE NOTES—Living the Runes

Key words:

Personal experiences/gleanings of Thurisaz's influence:

Concluding concepts or ideas on Thurisaz:

WEEK FOUR TRACKER: ANSUZ ᚨ, a

AN ANCESTRAL GOD

Inspirational Quote on Ansuz:

Initial concept or idea of Ansuz:

Ætt One; Ansuz ᚨ							
	M	T	W	TH	F	S	S
Fehu (ᚠ)							
Uruz (ᚢ)							
THurisaz (ᚦ)							
Ansuz (ᚨ)							
Raidho (ᚱ)							
Kenaz (ᚲ)							
Gebo (ᚷ)							
Wunjo (ᚹ)							

WEEK FOUR NOTES—Living the Runes

Key words:

Personal experiences/gleanings of Ansuz's influence:

Concluding concepts or ideas on Ansuz :

WEEK FIVE TRACKER: RAIDHO ᚱ, r

WAGON

Inspirational Quote on Raido:

Initial concept or idea of Raido:

Ætt One; Raido ᚱ							
	M	**T**	**W**	**TH**	**F**	**S**	**S**
Fehu (ᚠ)							
Uruz (ᚢ)							
THurisaz (ᚦ)							
Ansuz (ᚨ)							
Raidho (ᚱ)							
Kenaz (ᚲ)							
Gebo (ᚷ)							
Wunjo (ᚹ)							

WEEK FIVE NOTES—Living the Runes

Key words:

Personal experiences/gleanings of Raido's influence:

Concluding concepts or ideas on Raido:

WEEK SIX TRACKER: KENAZ ᚲ, k

TORCH

Inspirational Quote on Kenaz:

Initial concept or idea of Kenaz:

Ætt One; Kenaz ᚲ							
	M	**T**	**W**	**TH**	**F**	**S**	**S**
Fehu (ᚠ)							
Uruz (ᚢ)							
THurisaz (ᚦ)							
Ansuz (ᚨ)							
Raidho (ᚱ)							
Kenaz (ᚲ)							
Gebo (ᚷ)							
Wunjo (ᚹ)							

WEEK SIX NOTES—Living the Runes

Key words:

Personal experiences/gleanings of Kenaz's influence:

Concluding concepts or ideas on Kenaz:

WEEK SEVEN TRACKER: GEBO X, g

GIFT, HOSPITALITY

Inspirational Quote on Gebo:

Initial concept or idea of Gebo:

Ætt One; Gebo X							
	M	T	W	TH	F	S	S
Fehu (ᚠ)							
Uruz (ᚢ)							
THurisaz (ᚦ)							
Ansuz (ᚨ)							
Raidho (ᚱ)							
Kenaz (ᚲ)							
Gebo (ᚷ)							
Wunjo (ᚹ)							

WEEK SEVEN NOTES—Living the Runes

Key words:

Personal experiences/gleanings of Gebo's influence:

Concluding concepts or ideas on Gebo:

WEEK EIGHT TRACKER: WUNJO ᚹ, W

JOY

Inspirational Quote on Wunjo:

Initial concept or idea of Wunjo:

Ætt One; Wunjo ᚹ							
	M	T	W	TH	F	S	S
Fehu (ᚠ)							
Uruz (ᚢ)							
THurisaz (ᚦ)							
Ansuz (ᚨ)							
Raidho (ᚱ)							
Kenaz (ᚲ)							
Gebo (ᚷ)							
Wunjo (ᚹ)							

WEEK EIGHT NOTES—Living the Runes
Key words:

Personal experiences/gleanings of Wunjo's influence:

Concluding concepts or ideas on Wunjo :

WEEK NINE TRACKER: HAGALAZ ᚺ, h

HAIL

Inspirational Quote on Hagalaz:

Initial concept or idea of Hagalaz:

Ætt Two; Hagalaz ᚺ							
	M	**T**	**W**	**TH**	**F**	**S**	**S**
Hagalaz (ᚺ)							
Naudhiz (ᚾ)							
Isa (ᛁ)							
Jera (ᛃ)							
Eihwaz (ᛇ)							
Perthro (ᛈ)							
Elhaz (ᛉ)							
Sowilo (ᛋ)							

WEEK NINE NOTES—Living the Runes

Key words:

Personal experiences/gleanings of Hagalaz's influence:

Concluding concepts or ideas on Hagalaz:

WEEK TEN TRACKER: NAUDHIZ ᚾ, n

NEED

Inspirational Quote on Naudhiz:

Initial concept or idea of Naudhiz:

Ætt Two; Naudhiz ᚾ							
	M	**T**	**W**	**TH**	**F**	**S**	**S**
Hagalaz (ᚺ)							
Naudhiz (ᚾ)							
Isa (ᛁ)							
Jera (ᛃ)							
Eihwaz (ᛇ)							
Perthro (ᛈ)							
Elhaz (ᛉ)							
Sowilo (ᛊ)							

WEEK TEN NOTES—Living the Runes
Key words:

Personal experiences/gleanings of Naudhiz's influence:

Concluding concepts or ideas on Naudhiz:

WEEK ELEVEN TRACKER: ISA |, i

ICE

Inspirational Quote on Isa:

Initial concept or idea of Isa:

Ætt Two; Isa							
	M	**T**	**W**	**TH**	**F**	**S**	**S**
Hagalaz (ᚺ)							
Naudhiz (ᚾ)							
Isa (ᛁ)							
Jera (ᛃ)							
Eihwaz (ᛇ)							
Perthro (ᛈ)							
Elhaz (ᛉ)							
Sowilo (ᛊ)							

WEEK ELEVEN NOTES—Living the Runes
Key words:

Personal experiences/gleanings of Isa's influence:

Concluding concepts or ideas on Isa:

WEEK TWELVE TRACKER: JERA ᛃ, j

YEAR, HARVEST

Inspirational Quote on Jera:

Initial concept or idea of Jera:

Ætt Two; Jera ᛃ							
	M	**T**	**W**	**TH**	**F**	**S**	**S**
Hagalaz (ᚺ)							
Naudhiz (ᚾ)							
Isa (ᛁ)							
Jera (ᛃ)							
Eihwaz (ᛇ)							
Perthro (ᛈ)							
Elhaz (ᛉ)							
Sowilo (ᛊ)							

WEEK TWELVE NOTES—Living the Runes
Key words:

Personal experiences/gleanings of Jera's influence:

Concluding concepts or ideas on Jera:

WEEK THIRTEEN TRACKER: EIHWAZ ↓, e/i

YEW TREE

Inspirational Quote on Eihwaz:

Initial concept or idea of Eihwaz:

Ætt Two; Eihwaz ↓							
	M	T	W	TH	F	S	S
Hagalaz (ᚺ)							
Naudhiz (ᚾ)							
Isa (ᛁ)							
Jera (ᛃ)							
Eihwaz (↓)							
Perthro (ᛈ)							
Elhaz (ᛉ)							
Sowilo (ᛋ)							

WEEK THIRTEEN NOTES—Living the Runes
Key words:

Personal experiences/gleanings of Eihwaz's influence:

Concluding concepts or ideas on Eihwaz:

WEEK FOURTEEN TRACKER: PERTHRO ᛈ, p

DEVICE FOR CASTING LOTS

Inspirational Quote on Perthro:

Initial concept or idea of Perthro:

Ætt Two; Perthro ᛈ							
	M	**T**	**W**	**TH**	**F**	**S**	**S**
Hagalaz (ᚺ)							
Naudhiz (ᚾ)							
Isa (ᛁ)							
Jera (ᛃ)							
Eihwaz (ᛇ)							
Perthro (ᛈ)							
Elhaz (ᛉ)							
Sowilo (ᛋ)							

WEEK FOUTEEN NOTES—Living the Runes
Key words:

Personal experiences/gleanings of Perthro's influence:

Concluding concepts or ideas on Perthro:

WEEK FIFTEEN TRACKER: ELHAZ Υ, a/z

ELK, PROTECTION

Inspirational Quote on Elhaz:

Initial concept or idea of Elhaz:

Ætt Two; Elhaz Υ							
	M	**T**	**W**	**TH**	**F**	**S**	**S**
Hagalaz (N)							
Naudhiz ($\mathsf{\dagger}$)							
Isa (I)							
Jera ($\mathsf{\diamond}$)							
Eihwaz ($\mathsf{\Lambda}$)							
Perthro (K)							
Elhaz (Υ)							
Sowilo ($\mathsf{\varsigma}$)							

WEEK FIFTEEN NOTES—Living the Runes
Key words:

Personal experiences/gleanings of Elhaz's influence:

Concluding concepts or ideas on Elhaz:

WEEK SIXTEEN TRACKER: SOWILO ᛋ, S

SUN

Inspirational Quote on Sowilo:

Initial concept or idea of Sowilo:

Ætt Two; Sowilo ᛋ							
	M	**T**	**W**	**TH**	**F**	**S**	**S**
Hagalaz (ᚺ)							
Naudhiz (ᚾ)							
Isa (ᛁ)							
Jera (ᛃ)							
Eihwaz (ᛇ)							
Perthro (ᛈ)							
Elhaz (ᛉ)							
Sowilo (ᛋ)							

WEEK SIXTEEN NOTES—Living the Runes
Key words:

Personal experiences/gleanings of Sowilo's influence:

Concluding concepts or ideas on Sowilo:

WEEK SEVENTEEN TRACKER: TIWAZ ↑, t

THE GOD TYR

Inspirational Quote on Tiwaz:

Initial concept or idea of Tiwaz:

Ætt Three; Tiwaz ↑							
	M	T	W	TH	F	S	S
Tiwaz (↑)							
Berkano (ᛒ)							
Ehwaz (ᛖ)							
Mannaz (ᛗ)							
Laguz (ᛚ)							
Ingwaz (◇)							
Dagaz (ᛞ)							
Othala (ᛟ)							

WEEK SEVENTEEN NOTES—Living the Runes
Key words:

Personal experiences/gleanings of Tiwaz's influence:

Concluding concepts or ideas on Tiwaz:

WEEK EIGHTEEN TRACKER: BERKANO ᛒ, b

BIRCH GODDESS

Inspirational Quote on Berkano:

Initial concept or idea of Berkano:

Ætt Three; Berkano ᛒ							
	M	**T**	**W**	**TH**	**F**	**S**	**S**
Tiwaz (↑)							
Berkano (ᛒ)							
Ehwaz (ᛗ)							
Mannaz (ᛗ)							
Laguz (ᛚ)							
Ingwaz (◇)							
Dagaz (ᛞ)							
Othala (ᛟ)							

WEEK EIGHTTEEN NOTES—Living the Runes
Key words:

Personal experiences/gleanings of Berkano's influence:

Concluding concepts or ideas on Berkano:

WEEK NINETEEN TRACKER: EHWAZ M, e

HORSE

Inspirational Quote on Ehwaz:

Initial concept or idea of Ehwaz:

Ætt Three; Ehwaz M							
	M	**T**	**W**	**TH**	**F**	**S**	**S**
Tiwaz (↑)							
Berkano (ᛒ)							
Ehwaz (ᛗ)							
Mannaz (ᛘ)							
Laguz (ᛚ)							
Ingwaz (◇)							
Dagaz (ᛞ)							
Othala (ᛟ)							

WEEK NINETEEN NOTES—Living the Runes

Key words:

Personal experiences/gleanings of Ehwaz's influence:

Concluding concepts or ideas on Ehwaz:

WEEK TWENTY TRACKER: MANNAZ ᛗ, m

HUMAN

Inspirational Quote on Mannaz:

Initial concept or idea of Mannaz:

Ætt Three; Mannaz ᛗ							
	M	T	W	TH	F	S	S
Tiwaz (↑)							
Berkano (ᛒ)							
Ehwaz (ᛖ)							
Mannaz (ᛗ)							
Laguz (ᛚ)							
Ingwaz (◇)							
Dagaz (ᛞ)							
Othala (ᛟ)							

WEEK TWENTY NOTES—Living the Runes

Key words:

Personal experiences/gleanings of Mannaz's influence:

Concluding concepts or ideas on Mannaz:

WEEK TWENTY-ONE TRACKER: LAGUZ ᛚ,1

A BODY OF WATER

Inspirational Quote on Laguz:

Initial concept or idea of Laguz:

Ætt Three; Laguz ᛚ							
	M	**T**	**W**	**TH**	**F**	**S**	**S**
Tiwaz (ᛏ)							
Berkano (ᛒ)							
Ehwaz (ᛖ)							
Mannaz (ᛗ)							
Laguz (ᛚ)							
Ingwaz (◇)							
Dagaz (ᛞ)							
Othala (ᛟ)							

WEEK TWENTY-ONE NOTES—Living the Runes
Key words:

Personal experiences/gleanings of Laguz's influence:

Concluding concepts or ideas on Laguz:

WEEK TWENTY-TWO TRACKER: INGWAZ ◇, ng

THE GOD ING

Inspirational Quote on Ingwaz:

Initial concept or idea of Ingwaz:

Ætt Three; Ingwaz ◇							
	M	T	W	TH	F	S	S
Tiwaz (↑)							
Berkano (ᛒ)							
Ehwaz (ᛗ)							
Mannaz (ᛗ)							
Laguz (ᛚ)							
Ingwaz (◇)							
Dagaz (ᛞ)							
Othala (ᛟ)							

WEEK TWENTY-TWO NOTES—Living the Runes
Key words:

Personal experiences/gleanings of Ingwaz's influence:

Concluding concepts or ideas on Ingwaz:

WEEK TWENTY-THREE TRACKER: DAGAZ ᛞ, d

DAY

Inspirational Quote on Dagaz:

Initial concept or idea of Dagaz:

Ætt Three; Dagaz ᛞ							
	M	**T**	**W**	**TH**	**F**	**S**	**S**
Tiwaz (↑)							
Berkano (ᛒ)							
Ehwaz (ᛖ)							
Mannaz (ᛗ)							
Laguz (ᛚ)							
Ingwaz (◇)							
Dagaz (ᛞ)							
Othala (ᛟ)							

WEEK TWENTY-THREE NOTES—Living the Runes
Key words:

Personal experiences/gleanings of Dagaz's influence:

Concluding concepts or ideas on Dagaz:

WEEK TWENTY-FOUR TRACKER: OTHALA ⚷, O

ANCESTRAL PROPERTY

Inspirational Quote on Othala:

Initial concept or idea of Othala:

Ætt Three; Othala ⚷							
	M	T	W	TH	F	S	S
Tiwaz (↑)							
Berkano (ᛒ)							
Ehwaz (ᛖ)							
Mannaz (ᛗ)							
Laguz (ᛚ)							
Ingwaz (◇)							
Dagaz (ᛞ)							
Othala (⚷)							

WEEK TWENTY-FOUR NOTES—Living the Runes
Key words:

Personal experiences/gleanings of Othala's influence:

Concluding concepts or ideas on Othala:

Living the Runes
Twenty-Four Week Analysis of the Exercise

Living the Runes Analysis of the Exercise

Practical Application Assessment One-Week Journaling Exercise #5

Cumulative Assessment of Practical Application Exercises
One Week Exercise

Review, analyze, and evaluate your growth, maturity and working knowledge of each of the primary areas investigated—critical thinking, character improvement, small-group leadership, and operative runology.

Cumulative Assessment

Cumulative Assessment

CONCLUSTION
Einherjar—Knights of the Odinic Mysteries

In the reconstruction of Asatru, we should not be surprised to find metaphysical, mystical, or gnostic concepts within its myths and subsequent "spiritual" philosophy. Each year archeology reveals that the indigenous European tribes were not the barbarians they are portrayed as in ancient records. Gravesites and grave-ships reveal a very structured Norse religious belief system, reflecting a very complex psychological bond to both the natural world of Midgard and the metaphysical worlds of Yggdrasil.

Protecting this ancient Norse tradition are the "living deads" of Odin, the Einherjar. Each day they rise and hone their battle skills in "the uncreated place where the battle surges." These warriors are commissioned for eternity to protect Bifrost, that "royal road" to Asgard and they are ever attentive to the sound of the Gjallarhorn, that call from the Guardian Heimdall, which signals a threat to their tradition's safety.

217

At the end of each day, before they are welcomed to feast peacefully among the gods, their character is judged, not by any man, but by the Goddess Freya and Warlord Odin Themselves. The development of noble virtues, the conquest of vices, and the mastery over base passions has always been that ancient path to divinity. Along this path the Einherjar find the opportunity to uphold their warrior's oath while pursuing a wizard's wealth.

Ultimately, as depicted within our myths, these "commanders-of-one" and "peer-less" warriors are destined to become the Philosopher-Kings of themselves, ever striving to emulate both the Patriarch of their order Heimdall and their Vitki, All-Father Odin.

To quote again Joseph Campbell before I close, and as my literary "call to action," remember:

> It's important to live life with the experience, and therefore the knowledge, of its mystery and of your own mystery. This gives life a new radiance, a new harmony, a new splendor. Thinking in mythological terms helps to put you in accord with the inevitables of this vale of tears. You learn to recognize the positive values in what appear to be the negative moments and aspects of your life. The big question is whether you are going to be able to say a hearty yes to your adventure.[180]

APPENDIX: TOPICAL READING LIST

The resources listed here were referenced within Einherjar— Gnostic Warriors of the North: Way of the Einherjar, Vol. 1, and are arranged by subject/topic for the convenience of further study.

ASATRU

Linzie, Bil, *Drinking at the Well of Mimir: An Asatru Man's Meanderings Through the Last 30 Years*. Dec. 2000. Retrieved from http://www.heathengods.com/library/bil_linzie/well_of_ mimir.pdf.

———— *Germanic Spirituality*. July 2003. Retrieved from http://www.heathengods.com/library/bil_linzie/ germanic_spirituality.pdf.

———— *Investigating the Afterlife Concepts of the Norse Heathen: A Reconstructionist's Approach*. Dec. 2005. Retrieved from http://www.heathengods.com/library/bil_linzie/after_life _bil_linzie.pdf.

———— *Uncovering the Effects of Cultural Background on the Reconstruction of Ancient Worldviews*. March 2004. Retrieved from http://www.heathengods.com/library/bil_linzie/cultural_ background.pdf.

McNallen, Stephen A. *Ancestral Roots & Metagenetics*. Red Ice TV, published July 12, 2014. Retrieved from https://www.youtube.com/watch?v=B546mQQZ- sE&t=270s

———— *Asatru: A Native European Spirituality*. Nevada City: Runestone Press, 2015.

————— "Three decades of the Asatru Revival in America," in *Tyr: Myth—Culture—Tradition, Volume 2*, ed. Joshua Buckley and Michael Moynihan (Atlanta: Ultra Publishing, 2004/2008), 219.

McVan, Ron. *The Temple of Wotan: Holy Book of the Aryan Tribes*. St. Maries: Fourteen Word Press, 2000.

————— *Creed of Iron: Wotansvolk Wisdom* and *Temple of Wotan: Holy Book of the Aryan Tribes*. St. Maries: Fourteen Word Press, 1997.

Rayner, Dan. *Asatru Mindset & Reinvigorating the European Spirit*. Red Ice TV, published July 21, 2014. Retrieved from https://www.youtube.com/watch?v=j3KEbgdCBBA&t= 2217s

Robinson, B. A. "World Religions—Asatru: Norse Heathenism," *Ontario Consultants on Religious Tolerance*, 1997-2011. http://www.religioustolerance.org/asatru.htm.

Thorsson, Edred. *A Book of Troth*. Smithsville: Runa-Raven Press, 2003.

Wilton, Bryan. "Why the Opposition Doesn't Matter." ABN— Aesir Broadcasting Network. Published Oct. 28, 2016. Retrieved from https://soundcloud.com/aesirbroadcasting/abn-bryan-wilton-why-the-opposition-doesnt-matter-24.

C/K/QABALA

Barry, Kieren. *The Greek Qabalah: Alphabetic Mysticism and Numerology in the Ancient World*. York Beach: Samuel Weiser, Inc., 1999.

West, Shelly. *Kabbalistic Psychology*. Gnostic Warrior, published February 1, 2017. Retrieved from gnosticwarrior.com/shelly-west-2.html.

EDDIC LITERATURE

Bellows, Henry Adams. *The Poetic Edda*. The American Scandinavian Foundation, 1923.

Chisholm, James Allen. *The Eddas: The Keys to the Mysteries of the North*. Internet Archive (open source). Retrieved from https://archive.org/details/TheEddasTheKeysToTheMyst James AllenChisholm.

Larrington, Carolyne. *The Poetic Edda*. Oxford University Press, 1999.

Mackenzie, Donald A. *Teutonic Myth and Legend: An Introduction to the Eddas & Sagas, Beowolf, The Nibelungenlied, etc.* London: Gresham Publications, 1912.

Sturluson, Snorri. "Gylfaginning," *The Prose Edda*, trans. Arthur Gilchrist Brodeur. New York: The American Scandinavian Foundation, 1916.

ESOTERIC CHRISTIANITY

Besant, Annie. *Esoteric Christianity*. London: The Theosophical Publishing Society, 1905.

Janawitz, Naomi. *Magic in the Roman World: Pagans, Jews, and Christians*. New York: Routledge, 2001.

Simon. *Papal Magic: Occult Practices Within the Catholic Church*. New York: HarperCollins Publishers, Inc., 2007.

Smoley, Richard. *Inner Christianity: A Guide to the Esoteric Tradition.* Boston: Shambhala Publications, Inc., 2002.

ESOTERIC ORDERS

Case, Paul Foster. *Esoteric Secrets of Meditation & Magic.* Fraternity of the Hidden Light, 2008.

Flowers, Stephen E. *Fire and Ice—The History, Structure, and Rituals of Germany's Most Influential Modern Magical Order: The Brotherhood of Saturn.* St. Paul: Llewellyn Publications, 1994.

———— *Lords of the Left Hand Path: A History of Spiritual Dissent.* Smithville: Rune-Raven Press, 1997.

ESOTERIC PHILOSOPHY

Cleary, Collin. *What God Did Odin Worship.* Counter-Currents Publishing, 4/29/2011. Retrieved from http://www.counter-currents.com/2011/04/what-god-did-odin-worship/

Evans, C. S. *Pocket Dictionary of Apologetics & Philosophy of Religion.* Downers Grove: InterVarsity Press, 2002.

Foutz, Scott David "Universal Mysticism and the Christian Theistic Paradigm," *Quodlibet Journal* 1, no. 7, November 1999, http://www.quodlibet.net/articles/foutz-mystic.shtml.

Hofler, Otto. *Kultische Geheimbunde der Germanen.* Frankfurt: M. Diesterweg, 1934.

Levi, Eliphas. *Transcendental Magic, its Doctrine and Ritual,* trans. by A. E. Waite. London: George Redway, 1896.

Rubarth, Scott. "Stoic Philosophy of Mind." *Internet Encyclopedia of Philosophy: A Peer-Reviewed Academic Resource.* Retrieved from www.iep.utm.edu/stoicmind/

Steiner, Rudolf. *An Outline of Esoteric Science*, trans. Catherine E. Creeger. Hudson: Anthroposophic Press, 1997.

Swainson, W. P. *Jacob Boehm: The Teutonic Philosopher.* London: William Rider & Son, LTD., 1921.

Taliaferro, Charles. "Philosophy of Religion", *The Stanford Encyclopedia of Philosophy* (Winter 2014 Edition), Edward N. Zalta (ed.). Retrieved from https://plato.stanford.edu/entries/philosophy-religion/

Titchenell, Elsa-Brita. *The Masks of Odin: Wisdom of the Ancient Norse.* Theosophical University Press, 1985. Online edition retrieved from http://www.theosociety.org/pasadena/odin/odin-hp.htm.

FREEMASONRY

Carlile, Richard. *Manuel of Freemasonry.* Leeds: Celephais Press, 2005.

Hogan, Timothy W. "Gnostic Reflections in Freemasonry," *Freemason Information: A Web Magazine About Freemasonry.* Published by Greg Stewart, July 9, 2009. Retrieved from http://freemasoninformation.com/2009/07/gnostic-reflections-in-freemasonry/

Pike, Albert. *Morals and Dogma of the Ancient and Accepted Scottish Rite of Freemasonry.* Charleston, 1871. Retrieved from https://archive.org/details/moralsdogmaofanc00pikeiala.

GNOSTICISM

Bedard, Moe. *The Order of the Gnostics: Ancient Teachings for the Modern Gnostic.* Moeseo, Inc., 2015.

Hall, Manly P. *The Wisdom of the Knowing Ones.* Los Angeles: Philosophical Research Society, 2000.

Heindel, Max. *Parsifal: Wagner's Famous Mystic Music Drama.* "Rosicrucian Christianity", Series no. 12. Oceanside: The Rosicrucian Fellowship, 1909.

Hoeller, Stephan A. *Gnosticism: New Light on the Ancient Tradition of Inner Knowing.* Wheaton: Quest Books, 2002.

———— *The Gnostic Jung and the Seven Sermons to the Dead.* Wheaton: Quest Books, 1982.

Mead, G. R. S. trans. *Pistis Sophia.* The Gnostic Society Library, Gnostic Scriptures and Fragments. Retrieved from http://www.gnosis.org/library/pistis-sophia/index.htm

Weor, Samael Aun. *Introduction to Gnosis: Gnostic Methods for Today's World.* Glorian Publishing, 2009.

MODERN PSYCHOLOGY

Feldman, R. S. *Child Development,* 6/e XML Vitalsource eBook for EDMC (6th ed). Pearson Learning Solutions. Retrieved from http://digitalbookshelf.argosy.edu/books/9781256507079/id/ch09 box03

Gerrig, Richard J. *An Overview of Psychology: Its Past and Present, Your Future,* Custom Ed. Boston: Allyn & Bacon, 2009.

Gerrig, Richard J. and Zimbardo, Philip G. *Psychology and Life, Discovering Psychology Edition*. Boston: Allyn & Bacon, 2009.

Hogan, R. "The Superstitions of Everyday Life". *Behavioral and Brain Sciences,* *27*(6). Retrieved from http://search.proquest.com/docview/212219404? accountid=34899

Kenrick, Douglas. *Social Psychology: Goals in Interaction*, 4th ed. Boston: Allyn & Bacon, 2007.

King, D. Brett, *A History of Psychology: Ideas and Context*, 4th edition. Boston: Allyn & Bacon, 2009.

Mazur, J. (2005). Learning and Behavior [VitalSouce bookshelf version]. Retrieved from http://digitalbook shelf.argosy.edu/books/0558220231

Meyer, J. and Land, R. *Threshold Concepts and Troublesome Knowledge: Linkages to Ways of Thinking and Practicing Within the Disciplines*, 2003. Retrieved from: www.etl.tla.ed.ac.uk/docs/ETLreport4.pdf

Santrock, John W. *Life-Span Development*, 12th ed. New York: McGraw-Hill Higher Education, 2009.

Weimer, Maryellen. "Threshold Concepts: Portals to New Ways of Thinking," in *Faculty Focus: Higher Ed Teaching Strategies from Magna Publications*, November 7, 2014. Retrieved from www.facultyfocus.com/articles/teaching-and-learning/threshold-concepts-portals-new-ways-thinking/

MYTHOLOGY

Arvidsson, Stefan. *Aryan Idols: Indo-European Mythology as Ideology and Science*, trans. Sonia Wichmann. Chicago: University of Chicago Press, 2006.

Campbell, Joseph. *The Power of Myth with Bill Moyers*. New York: MJF Books, 1988.

Davidson, H. R. Ellis. *Gods & Myths of Northern Europe*. London: Penguin Books Ltd, 1990.

Daly, Kathleen N. *Norse Mythology A to Z*. New York: Chelsea House, 2010.

Graves, Kersey. *The World's Sixteen Crucified Saviors*, retrieved from http://www.sacred-texts.com/bib/cv/wscs/index.htm

Guerber, H. A. *Myths of Northern Lands*. New York: American Book Co., 1895.

Lindow, John. *Handbook of Norse Mythology*. Santa Barbara: ABC-CLIO, Inc., 2001.

Matasouie, Ranko. *A Reader in Comparative Indo-European Religion*. Zageb: University of Zageb, 2010.

McCoy, Dan. *The Lore of Destiny: The Sacred and the Profane in Germanic Polytheism* (2013); *Norse Mythology for Smart People* (2016). Retrieved from http://norse-mythology.org.

Orchard, Andy. *Dictionary of Norse Myth and Legend*. Cassell, 1997.

Rydberg, Viktor. *Teutonic Mythology: Gods and Goddesses of the Northland*. Vol. 1-3. New York: Norrœna Society, 1907.

Simek, Rudolf. *Dictionary of Northern Mythology*, trans. by Angela Hall. D.S. Brewer, 2007.

Steiner, Rudolf. *Angels, Archangels of the Folk and Myths of Northern Europe*. Lecture 1, 1919; published 2015. Retrieved from https://www.youtube.com/watch?v=frw0uuMKl-I

OCCULT PSYCHOLOGY

Hughes, K. (2011). Examiner.com. *Ritual, Psychology, Carl Jung and Archetypes*. Retrieved from http://www.examiner.com/article/ritual-psychology-carl-jung-and-archetypes on April 8, 2013

Hulse, David Allen. *New Dimensions for the Cube of Space: The Path of Initiation Revealed by the Tarot upon the Qabalistic Cube*. York Beach: Samuel Weiser, Inc., 2000.

Jung, Carl. *Essay on Wotan* [First published as WOTAN, Neue Schweizer Rundschau (Zurich). n.s., III (March, 1936), 657-69. Republished in Aufsatze Zurzeitgeschichte (Zurich, 1946), 1-23. Trans. by Barbara Hannah in Essays on Contemporary Events (London, 1947), 1-16; this version has been consulted. Motto, trans. by H.C. Roberts:] Retrieved from http://www.philosopher.eu/others-writings/essay-on-wotan-w-nietzsche-c-g-jung/

——— *Psychology and Religion*. New York: Routledge, 2008.

Tyson, Donald. New Millennium Magic: A Complete System of Self-Realization. St. Paul: Llewellyn Publications, 1996.

Waite, Arthur Edward. *The Way of Divine Union*. London: William Rider & Son, Ltd., 1915.

PAGANISM

De Benoise, Alain. *On Being a Pagan*, trans. Joh Graham, ed. Greg Johnson, pref. Stephen Edred Flowers. Atlanta: ULTRA, 2004.

Krasskova, Galina. *Exploring the Northern Tradition: A Guide to the Gods, Lore, Rites, and Celebrations from the Norse, German, and Anglo-Saxon Traditions.* Franklin Lakes: The Career Press, Inc., 2005.

PASTORAL COUNSELING

American Association of Pastoral Counselors (2012). *Code of Ethics.* Retrieved from http://aapc.org/Default.aspx?ssid=74&NavPTypeId=1161

American Counseling Association (2005). *Code of Ethics and Standards of Practice.* Retrieved from http://www.counseling.org/Resources/aca-code-of-ethics.pdf

American Psychological Association. (2010). *American Psychological Association: Ethical Principles of Psychologists and Code of Conduct.* Retrieved from http://www.apa.org/ethics/code/principles.pdf

RELIGIOUS EDUCATION

Barnes, L. P. and Kay, W. K. "Developments in Religious Education in England and Wales (Part 2): Methodology, Politics, Citizenship and School Performance," *Themelios* 25, no. 3. 2000.

Flowers, Stephen E *Restoring the Indo-European Religion.* Red Ice TV, published March 16, 2016. Retrieved from https://www.youtube.com/watch?v=VomiUEsqvAg

Hood, Ralph W., Jr. "Psychology of Religion," encyclopedia of Religion and Society, William H. Swatos (ed.). Retrieved from http://www.hirr.hartsem.edu/ency/Psychology.htm

Lincoln, Bruce. *Priests, Warriors, and Cattle: A Study in the Ecology of Religions.* Berkeley and Los Angeles: University of California Press, 1981.

Morris, Charles. *Aryan Sun-Myths: The Origin of Religions.* New York: Nims and Knight, 1889.

Patheos Online Religious Library: *South America.* http://www.patheos.com/Library/South-American

PBS. *From Jesus to Christ.* Frontline series, 4 parts, April, 1998. Full program with student and teacher's guide retrieved from http://www.pbs.org/wgbh/pages/frontline/shows/religion/watch/

Rees, T. "God," *The International Standard Bible Encyclopaedia*, 5 vols., ed. J. Orr, J. L. Nuelsen, E. Y. Mullins, & M. O. Evans. Chicago: The Howard-Severance Company, 1915.

Tisdall, W. S. C. "Comparative Religion," *The International Standard Bible Encyclopaedia*, 5 vols., ed. J. Orr, J. L. Nuelsen, E. Y. Mullins, & M. O. Evans. Chicago: The Howard-Severance Company, 1915.

Tylor, Edward Burnett. *Primitive Culture: Research into the Development of Mythology, Philosophy, Religion, Language, Art, and Custom.* New York: G. P. Putnam's Sons, 1920.

RUNOLOGY

Antonsen, Elmer H. "On the Mythological Interpretation of the Oldest Runic Inscriptions," in *Languages and Cultures: Studies in Honor of Edgar C. Polome*. Mohammard ali Jazayy and Werner Winter, eds. New York: Mouton de Gruyter, 1988.

Flowers, Stephen E "Toward an Archaic Germanic Psychology," in *Journal of Indo-European Studies*. Austin, University of Texas, n.d.

Thorsson, Edred. *ALU: An Advanced Guide to Operative Runology*. San Francisco: Weiser, 2012.

———— *Northern Magic: Rune Mysteries and Shamanism*. Woodbury: Llewellyn Publications, 2005.

———— *Runelore: A Handbook of Esoteric Runology*. York Beach: Weiser, 1987.

SYMBOLISM

Cooke, Bernard and Macy, Gary. *Christian Symbol and Ritual: An Introduction*. New York: Oxford University Press, 2005.

Inman, Thomas. *Ancient Pagan and Modern Christian Symbolism*. New York: J. W. Bouton, 1884.

Russell, James C. *The Germanization of Early Medieval Christianity: A Sociohistorical Approach to Religious Transformation*. New York: Oxford University Press, 1994.

Semetsky, Inna. *The Edusemiotics of Images: Essays on the Art-Science of Tarot*. Boston: Sense Publishers, 2013.

TEXTURAL CRITICISM

Barton, John. *The Cambridge Companion to Biblical Interpretation.* New York: Cambridge University Press, 1998.

Brand, Chad, et al., eds., "Hermetic Literature," *Holman Illustrated Bible Dictionary.* Nashville, TN: Holman Bible Publishers, 2003.

Callahan, Tim. *Secret Origins of the Bible.* Altadena: Millennium Press, 2002.

DeMaris, Richard E. *The New Testament in its Ritual World.* New York: Routledge, 2008.

Fee, Gordon and Stuart, Douglas. *How to Read the Bible for all its Worth.* Grand Rapids: Zondervan, 2003.

Gunther, Hans F. K. *The Religious Attitude of the Indo-Europeans*, Vivian Bird, trans. London: Clair Press, 1963.

Kittel, Gerhard. (ed.) *Theological Dictionary of the New Testament.* Grand Rapids: Eerdmans, 1964.

Nordgren, Ingemar. *The Well Spring of the Goths: About the Gothic Peoples in the Nordic Countries and on the Continent.* New York: iUniverse, Inc., 2004.

Wilton, Bryan. "Tacitus on the Germans," ABN—Aesir Broadcasting Network. Published January 18, 2017. Retrieved from https://soundcloud.com/aesirbroadcasting/abn-bryan-wilton-tacitus-on-the-germans-53

VEDIC LITERATURE

Frawley, David. *Wisdom of the Ancient Seers: Mantras of the Rig Veda.* Salt Lake City: Passage Press, 1992.

Pike, Albert. *Indo-Aryan Deities and Worship—As Contained in the Rig Veda.* Louisville: Standard Printing Co., 1930.

ENDNOTES

[1] One of my favorite film quotes. *Thor*, directed by Kenneth Branagh (Paramount Pictures, 2011). DVD release Sept. 13, 2011.

[2] St. Maries: Fourteen Word Press, 2000. The opening statement is adopted from "Rite of the Einherjar Warrior Initiation" from *The Temple of Wotan*, 368.

[3] Having become a contemporary statistic, I found myself aligning with Co-mason Annie Besant, who, over a century ago, wrote: "Christianity, having lost its mystic and esoteric teaching, is losing its hold on a large number of the more highly educated, and the partial revival during the past few years is coincident with the reintroduction of some mystic teaching. It is patent to every student of the closing forty years of the last century, that crowds of thoughtful and moral people have slipped away from the churches, because the teachings they received there outraged their intelligence and shocked their moral sense. It is idle to pretend that the widespread agnosticism of this period had its root either in lack of morality or in deliberate crookedness of mind. Everyone who carefully studies the phenomena presented will admit that men of strong intellect have been driven out of Christianity by the crudity of the religious ideas set before them, the contradictions in the authoritative teachings, the views as to God, man, and the universe that no trained intelligence could possibly admit. Nor can it be said that any kind of moral degradation lay at the root of the revolt against the dogmas of the Church. The rebels were not too bad for their religion; on the contrary, it was the religion that was too bad

for them. The rebellion against popular Christianity was due to the awakening and the growth of conscience; it was the conscience that revolted, as well as the intelligence, against teachings dishonoring to God and man alike, that represented God as a tyrant, and man as essentially evil, gaining salvation by slavish submission." *Esoteric Christianity*, originally published in 1905 by The Theosophical Publishing Society. A Project Gutenberg Ebook. Release date: Oct. 16, 2008. EBook #26938, p.26.

[4] Gnostic philosophy is expressed within the world's wisdom traditions from as far back as the teachings of ancient Persia, the Pythagoreans, and Neo-Platonists, through the magical traditions of the Middle Ages, and into the contemporary thoughts of Jacob Boehme, Carl Jung and Rudolf Steiner as well as the systems of the Rosicrucians and Freemasons. Gnostic thought often portrays the universe as embodying an endless battle between the opposing forces of order and harmony with those of discourse and chaos. Physical space and time is held in gnostic thought as that primary obstacle to humanity's ability in recognizing its divine character and inherent nature. Subsequently, foundational to gnostic thought is humanity's unlimited, i.e. omnipotent, potential; and, the purpose of any true wisdom school or mystical order then would be to instruct its initiates in methods and techniques for experiencing that inner, core nature where the only god they will every meet is enthroned. For an introduction to gnostic philosophy and Gnosticism in general see Manly P. Hall, *The Wisdom of the Knowing Ones* (Los Angeles: Philosophical Research Society, 2000); Rudolf Steiner, *An Outline of Esoteric Science*, trans. Catherine E. Creeger (Hudson: Anthroposophic Press, 1997); Samael Aun Weor, *Introduction to Gnosis: Gnostic Methods for Today's World* (Brooklyn: Glorian Publishing, 2009); Stephan A. Hoeller, *Gnosticism: New Light*

on the Ancient Tradition of Inner Knowing (Wheaton: Quest Books, 2002); *The Gnostic Jung and the Seven Sermons to the Dead* (Wheaton: Quest Books, 1982).

⁵ For those interested in my particular perspective on Asatru and the Asatru Folk movement I would recommend the following material: Bil Linzie, *Drinking at the Well of Mimir: An Asatru Man's Meanderings Through the Last 30 Years* (Dec. 8, 2000); Stephen A. McNallen, *Asatru: A Native European Spirituality* (Nevada City: Runestone Press, 2015); Ron McVan, *Creed of Iron: Wotansvolk Wisdom* and *Temple of Wotan: Holy Book of the Aryan Tribes* (St. Maries: Fourteen Word Press, 1997, 2000); Edred Thorsson, *A Book of Troth* (Smithsville: Runa-Raven Press, 2003).

⁶ *Angels, Archangels of the Folk and Myths of Northern Europe* Lecture 1, 1919; published 2015. Retrieved from https://www.youtube.com/watch?v=frw0uuMKl-I

⁷ For further study in this area see John Barton, *The Cambridge Companion to Biblical Interpretation* (New York: Cambridge University Press, 1998). Gordon Fee and Douglas Stuart, *How to Read the Bible for all its Worth* (Grand Rapids: Zondervan, 2003).

⁸ Patheos Online Religious Library: *South America.* http://www.patheos.com/Library/South-American

⁹ Donald A. Mackenzie, *Teutonic Myth and Legend: An Introduction to the Eddas & Sagas, Beowolf, The Nibelungenlied, etc.* (London: Gresham Publications, 1912); Hans F. K. Gunther, *The Religious Attitude of the Indo-Europeans*, Vivian Bird, trans. (London: Clair Press, 1963); H. R. Ellis Davidson, *Gods & Myths of Northern Europe* (London: Penguin books Ltd, 1990); Ranko Matasouie, *A Reader in Comparative Indo-European Religion* (Zageb: University of Zageb, 2010); Stephen A. McNallen, *Asatru: a Native European Spirituality* (Nevada City: Runestone Press, 2015), 191; Viktor Rydberg,

Teutonic Mythology: Gods and Goddesses of the Northland (New York: Norrœna Society, 1907).

[10] Albert Pike, *Indo-Aryan Deities and Worship—As Contained in the Rig Veda* (Louisville: Standard Printing Co., 1930); Charles Morris, *Aryan Sun-Myths: The Origin of Religions* (New York: Nims and Knight, 1889); David Frawley, *Wisdom of the Ancient Seers: Mantras of the Rig Veda* (Salt Lake City: Passage Press, 1992); Stefan Arvidsson, *Aryan Idols: Indo-European Mythology as Ideology and Science*, trans. Sonia Wichmann (Chicago: University of Chicago Press, 2006).

[11] Dan Rayner, *Asatru Mindset & Reinvigorating the European Spirit.* Red Ice TV, published July 21, 2014. Retrieved from https://www.youtube.com/watch?v=j3KEbgdCBBA&t=2217s; Edred Thorsson, *ALU: An Advanced Guide to Operative Runology* (San Francisco: Weiser, 2012) 145-161; Moe Bedard, *The Order of the Gnostics: Ancient Teachings for the Modern Gnostic* (Moeseo, Inc., 2015); Stephen E. Flowers, *Restoring the Indo-European Religion.* Red Ice TV, published March 16, 2016. Retrieved from https://www.youtube.com/watch?v=VomiUEsqvAg; Stephen A. McNallen, *Ancestral Roots & Metagenetics.* Red Ice TV, published July 12, 2014. Retrieved from https://www.youtube.com/watch?v= B546mQQZ-sE&t=270s; *Asatru: A Native European Spirituality* (Nevada City: Runestone Press, 2015), 76-83.

[12] *Pistis Sophia*, retrieved from http://www.gnosis.org/library/pistis-sophia/index.htm, Biblical text from the Gospel of Luke, 15: 11-32; Max Heindel, *Parsifal: Wagner's Famous Mystic Music Drama*, "Rosicrucian Christianity", Series no. 12 (Oceanside: The Rosicrucian Fellowship, 1909) 8, 13; Richard Carlile, *Manuel of Freemasonry* (Leeds: Celephais Press, 2005); *Star Wars*, written and directed by George Lucas (1977, Lucasfilm Ltd., 20th Century Fox Home Entertainment, 2011), Blu-ray Disc; *The Matrix*, written and

directed by The Wachawski Brothers (1999, Warner Bros., Warner Home Entertainment, 2009), Blu-ray Disc.

[13] Dan Rayner, *Asatru Mindset & Reinvigorating the European Spirit*. Red Ice TV, published July 21, 2014. Retrieved from https://www.youtube.com/watch?v=j3KEbgdCBBA&t=2217s; Edred Thorsson, *ALU: An Advanced Guide to Operative Runology* (San Francisco: Weiser, 2012) 145-161; Moe Bedard, *The Order of the Gnostics: Ancient Teachings for the Modern Gnostic* (Moeseo, Inc., 2015); Stephen E. Flowers, *Restoring the Indo-European Religion*. Red Ice TV, published March 16, 2016. Retrieved from https://www.youtube.com/watch?v=VomiUEsqvAg; Stephen A. McNallen, *Ancestral Roots & Metagenetics*. Red Ice TV, published July 12, 2014. Retrieved from https://www.youtube.com/watch?v= B546mQQZ-sE&t=270s; *Asatru: A Native European Spirituality* (Nevada City: Runestone Press, 2015), 76-83.

[14] Shelly West, *Kabbalistic Psychology*, Gnostic Warrior, published February 1, 2017. Retrieved from gnosticwarrior.com/shelly-west-2.html.

[15] American Association of Pastoral Counselors (2012). Code of Ethics Retrieved from http://aapc.org/Default.aspx?ssid= 74&NavPTypeId=1161; American Counseling Association (2005). Code of ethics and standards of practice. Retrieved from http://www.counseling.org/Resources/aca-code-of-ethics.pdf American Psychological Association. (2010). American psychological association: Ethical principles of psychologists and code of conduct. Retrieved from http://www.apa.org/ethics/code/principles.pdf

[16] St. Paul: Llewellyn Publications, 1996, 309.

[17] *ALU: An Advanced Guide to Operative Runology* (San Francisco, CA: Weiser Books, 2012), 166.

[18] *Essay on Wotan* [First published as WOTAN, Neue Schweizer Rundschau (Zurich). n.s., III (March, 1936), 657-69. Republished in

Aufsatze Zurzeitgeschichte (Zurich, 1946), 1-23. Trans. by Barbara Hannah in Essays on Contemporary Events (London, 1947), 1-16; this version has been consulted. Motto, trans. by H.C. Roberts:] Retrieved from http://www.philosopher.eu/others-writings/essay-on-wotan-w-nietzsche-c-g-jung/

[19] "Three decades of the Asatru Revival in America," in *Tyr: Myth—Culture—Tradition, Volume 2,* ed. Joshua Buckley and Michael Moynihan (Atlanta: Ultra Publishing, 2004/2008), 219.

[20] B. A. Robinson, "World Religions—Asatru: Norse Heathenism," *Ontario Consultants on Religious Tolerance*, 1997-2011. http://www.religioustolerance.org/asatru.htm.

[21] Ibid.; Edred Thorsson, *A Book of Troth* (Smithville: Raven-Runa Press, 2003), 2.

[22] Smithville: Raven-Runa Press, 2003, 2.

[23] Edred Thorsson, *A Book of Troth* (Smithville: Raven-Runa Press, 2003), 2; Stephen A. McNallen, *Asatru: a Native European Spirituality* (Nevada City: Runestone Press, 2015), 2.

[24] B. A. Robinson, "World Religions, Asatru: Norse Heathenism," *Ontario Consultants on Religious Tolerance*, 1997-2011. http://www.religioustolerance.org/asatru.htm.

[25] Joseph Campbell, *The Power of Myth with Bill Moyers* (New York: MJF Books, 1988), 206.

[26] Ibid.

[27] *Essay on Wotan* [First published as WOTAN, Neue Schweizer Rundschau (Zurich). n.s., III (March, 1936), 657-69. Republished in Aufsatze Zurzeitgeschichte (Zurich, 1946), 1-23. Trans. by Barbara Hannah in Essays on Contemporary Events (London, 1947), 1-16; this version has been consulted. Motto, trans. by H.C. Roberts:] Retrieved from http://www.philosopher.eu/others-writings/essay-on-wotan-w-nietzsche-c-g-jung/

[28] Directed by Sturla Gunnarsson (Truly Indie).

[29] Directed by Nora Ephron (Turner Pictures/New Line Cinema).

[30] Contemporary thought, from online "gaming" communities to prison gangs, regarding the true nature of the Einherjar of Odin and their mission is as misunderstood and stereotyped as Ms. Winter's expectations of the archangel Michael. In the case of the Einherjar however, it is the "halos" and "inner light" that has been forgotten. Though we would naturally expect service and duty to others, self-sacrifice, and the quest for knowledge to be at the center of anyone's life that truly emulated Allfather Odin, the Einherjar—Odin's Commanders of One—are more often than not understood as simple foot-soldiers, "grunts", and even bullies of the folk rather than being recognized, remembered, and celebrated as the Priest-Kings, Demi-gods, and Heroes which they represented to our ancestors

[31] Kabala, Cabala, or Qabala are all variations of the word כבל (KBL), the Hebrew word for *tradition* used to indicate the *traditional wisdom* passed on from mentor to initiate. The variations in spelling indicate the gnostic line from which the tradition stems. *Kabala* designates a more Jewish-gnostic tradition. *Cabala* designates a Christian-gnostic influence. Use of the word *Qabala* is typically indicative of a more Hermetic-gnostic philosophy. For clarity throughout the text, I shall use the spelling appropriate for the tradition or influence being discussed at that particular moment.

[32] Dan Rayner, *Asatru Mindset & Reinvigorating the European Spirit*. Red Ice TV, published July 21, 2014. Retrieved from https://www.youtube.com/watch?v=j3KEbgdCBBA&t=2217s; Edred Thorsson, *ALU: An Advanced Guide to Operative Runology* (San Francisco: Weiser, 2012) 145-161; Moe Bedard, *The Order of the*

Gnostics: Ancient Teachings for the Modern Gnostic (Moeseo, Inc., 2015); Stephen E. Flowers, *Restoring the Indo-European Religion*. Red Ice TV, published March 16, 2016. Retrieved from https://www.youtube.com/watch?v=VomiUEsqvAg; Stephen A. McNallen, *Ancestral Roots & Metagenetics*. Red Ice TV, published July 12, 2014. Retrieved from https://www.youtube.com/watch?v=B546mQQZ-sE&t=270s; *Asatru: A Native European Spirituality* (Nevada City: Runestone Press, 2015), 76-83.

[33] L. P. Barnes and W. K. Kay, "Developments in Religious Education in England and Wales (Part 2): Methodology, Politics, Citizenship and School Performance," *Themelios* 25, no. 3 (2000): 5-16.

[34] Stephen A. McNallen, "Three decades of the Asatru Revival in America," in *Tyr: Myth—Culture—Tradition*, 2nd ed. Joshua Buckley and Michael Moynihan (Atlanta: Ultra Publishing, 2004/2008), 218.

[35] Ibid. See also Alain de Benoist, *On Being a Pagan*, trans. Joh Graham, ed. Greg Johnson, pref. Stephen Edred Flowers (Atlanta: ULTRA, 2004).

[36] Stephen A. McNallen, "Three decades of the Asatru Revival in America," in *Tyr: Myth—Culture—Tradition*, 2nd ed. Joshua Buckley and Michael Moynihan (Atlanta: Ultra Publishing, 2004/2008), 211; *Asatru: A Native European Spirituality* (Nevada City: Runestone Press, 2015), 66.

[37] Annie Besant, *Esoteric Christianity*. (London: The Theosophical Publishing Society, 1905); Richard E. DeMaris, *The New Testament in its Ritual World* (New York: Routledge, 2008); Richard Smoley, *Inner Christianity: A Guide to the Esoteric Tradition* (Boston: Shambhala Publications, Inc., 2002); Simon, *Papal Magic: Occult Practices Within the Catholic Church* (New York: HarperCollins Publishers, Inc., 2007).

[38] Arthur Edward Waite, *The Way of Divine Union* (London: William Rider & Son, Ltd., 1915); Bernard Cooke and Gary Macy, *Christian Symbol and Ritual: An Introduction* (New York: Oxford University Press, 2005); Naomi Janawitz, *Magic in the Roman World: Pagans, Jews, and Christians* (New York: Routledge, 2001).

[39] *ALU: An Advanced Guide to Operative Runology.* (San Francisco: Weiser, 2012), 160.

[40] Rudolf Steiner, *An Outline of Esoteric Science* (New York: Anthroposophic Press, 1997).

[41] J. Meyer and R. Land, *Threshold Concepts and Troublesome Knowledge: Linkages to Ways of Thinking and Practicing Within the Disciplines,* 2003. Retrieved from :www.etl.tla.ed.ac.uk/docs/ETLreport4.pdf

[42] Ibid.

[43] Maryellen Weimer, *Threshold Concepts: Portals to New Ways of Thinking,* in Faculty Focus: Higher Ed Teaching Strategies from Magna Publications, November 7, 2014. Retrieved from www.facultyfocus. com/articles/teaching-and-learning/threshold-concepts-portals-new-ways-thinking/

[44] Frontline series, 4 parts, April, 1998. Full program with student and teacher's guide retrieved from http://www.pbs.org/wgbh/pages/frontline/shows/religion/watch/

[45] James C. Russell, *The Germanization of Early Medieval Christianity: A Sociohistorical Approach to Religious Transformation* (New York: Oxford University Press, 1994); Thomas Inman, *Ancient Pagan and Modern Christian Symbolism* (New York: J. W. Bouton, 1884); Tim Callahan, *Secret Origins of the Bible* (Altadena: Millennium Press, 2002).

[46] Carl Jung, *Psychology and Religion* (New York: Routledge, 2008); Elmer H. Antonsen, *On the Mythological Interpretation of the Oldest Runic Inscriptions,* in Languages and Cultures: Studies in Honor of Edgar

C. Polome. Mohammard ali Jazayy and Werner Winter, eds. (New York: Mouton de Gruyter, 1988); Inna Semetsky, *The Edusemiotics of Images: Essays on the Art-Science of Tarot* (Boston: Sense Publishers, 2013); Paul Foster Case, *Esoteric Secrets of Meditation & Magic* (Fraternity of the Hidden Light, 2008); Stephen E. Flowers, *Toward an Archaic Germanic Psychology*, in Journal of Indo-European Studies (Austin, University of Texas, n.d.).

[47] Kieren Barry, *The Greek Qabalah: Alphabetic Mysticism and Numerology in the Ancient World* (York Beach: Samuel Weiser, Inc., 1999); Ron McVan, *The Temple of Wotan: Holy Book of the Aryan Tribes* (St. Maries: 14 Word Press, 2000), 30; Stephen E. Flowers, *Lords of the Left Hand Path: A History of Spiritual Dissent* (Smithville: Rune-Raven Press, 1997).

[48] The Sefer Yetzirah: Cube of Space—The Dimensions of Consciousness (n.d.). Retrieved from www.psyche.com/psyche.

[49] Ibid.; David Allen Hulse, *New Dimensions for the Cube of Space: The Path of Initiation Revealed by the Tarot upon the Qabalistic Cube* (York Beach: Samuel Weiser, Inc., 2000), 127.

[50] *Morals and Dogma of the Ancient and Accepted Scottish Rite of Freemasonry* (Charleston, 1871), 5, 16. Retrieved from https://archive.org/details/moralsdogmaofanc00pikeiala.

[51] 1 Ki. 8; 2 Ch. 3; Rev. 21.

[52] David Allen Hulse, *New Dimensions for the Cube of Space: The Path of Initiation Revealed by the Tarot upon the Qabalistic Cube* (York Beach: Samuel Weiser, Inc., 2000).

[53] Ibid.

[54] Ibid.

[55] Ibid.

[56] Scott Rubarth, *Stoic Philosophy of Mind*. Internet Encyclopedia of Philosophy: A Peer-Reviewed Academic Resource. Retrieved from

www.iep.utm.edu/stoicmind/; The Sefer Yetzirah: Cube of Space—The Dimensions of Consciousness (n.d.). Retrieved from www.psyche.com/psyche.

[57] Edred Thorsson, *Runelore: A Handbook of Esoteric Runology* (York Beach: Weiser, 1987), 168-173; *Northern Magic: Rune Mysteries and Shamanism* (Woodbury: Llewellyn Publications, 2005), 19-25.

[58] Edred Thorsson, *Runelore: A Handbook of Esoteric Runology* (York Beach: Weiser, 1987), 168-171.

[59] Since the center is recognized twice, as a starting and a concluding point, there are exactly 32 "Paths of Wisdom" illustrated within the depicted Norse Psycho-Cosmological Cube, something that even the Qabalah fails to provide within the construct of its "Cube of Space."

[60] Edred Thorsson. *ALU: An Advanced Guide to Operative Runology.* (San Francisco: Weiser, 2012), 160.

[61] "Universal Mysticism and the Christian Theistic Paradigm," *Quodlibet Journal* 1, no. 7, November 1999, http://www.quodlibet.net/articles/foutz-mystic.shtml.

[62] W. S. C. Tisdall, "Comparative Religion," *The International Standard Bible Encyclopaedia*, 5 vols., ed. J. Orr, J. L. Nuelsen, E. Y. Mullins, & M. O. Evans (Chicago: The Howard-Severance Company, 1915), 692.

[63] Ibid.

[64] T. Rees, "God," *The International Standard Bible Encyclopaedia*, 5 vols., ed. J. Orr, J. L. Nuelsen, E. Y. Mullins, & M. O. Evans (Chicago: The Howard-Severance Company, 1915), 1252.

[65] Richard J. Gerrig and Philip G. Zimbardo, *Psychology and Life, Discovering Psychology Edition*, (Boston: Allya and Bacon, 2009), 552.

[66] W. S. C. Tisdall, "Comparative Religion," *The International Standard Bible Encyclopaedia*, 5 vols., ed. J. Orr, J. L. Nuelsen, E. Y.

Mullins, & M. O. Evans (Chicago: The Howard-Severance Company, 1915)

[67] Ibid.

[68] C. S. Evans, *Pocket Dictionary of Apologetics & Philosophy of Religion* (Downers Grove: InterVarsity Press, 2002), 11, 44-45.

[69] W. S. C. Tisdall, "Comparative Religion," *The International Standard Bible Encyclopaedia*, 5 vols., ed. J. Orr, J. L. Nuelsen, E. Y. Mullins, & M. O. Evans (Chicago: The Howard-Severance Company, 1915).

[70] Scott David Foutz, "Universal Mysticism and the Christian Theistic Paradigm," *Quodlibet Journal* 1, no. 7, November 1999, http://www.quodlibet.net/articles/foutz-mystic.shtml.

[71] Ibid.

[72] Ibid.

[73] W. S. C. Tisdall, "Comparative Religion," *The International Standard Bible Encyclopaedia*, 5 vols., ed. J. Orr, J. L. Nuelsen, E. Y. Mullins, & M. O. Evans (Chicago: The Howard-Severance Company, 1915).

[74] Ibid

[75] Gerhard Kittel, Geoffrey W. Bromiley, and Gerhard Friedrich, eds., *Theological Dictionary of the New Testament* (Grand Rapids: Eerdmans, 1964), 772.

[76] W. S. C. Tisdall, "Comparative Religion," *The International Standard Bible Encyclopaedia*, 5 vols., ed. J. Orr, J. L. Nuelsen, E. Y. Mullins, & M. O. Evans (Chicago: The Howard-Severance Company, 1915).

[77] Gerhard Kittel, *Theological Dictionary of the New Testament*, 255.

[78] Ibid.

[79] W. S. C. Tisdall, "Comparative Religion," *The International Standard Bible Encyclopaedia*, Vol. 1–5, ed. J. Orr, J. L. Nuelsen, E. Y.

Mullins, & M. O. Evans (Chicago: The Howard-Severance Company, 1915), 692.

[80] Chad Brand, Charles Draper, Archie England, et al., eds., "Hermetic Literature," *Holman Illustrated Bible Dictionary* (Nashville, TN: Holman Bible Publishers, 2003), 752.

[81] In Pistis Sophia we have a description of the path of the soul from chaos to the inheritance on high. Cf. G. Bertram, Art. "Erhöhung," RAC, VI, 22–43.

[82] Edward Burnett Tylor, *Primitive Culture: Research into the Development of Mythology, Philosophy, Religion, Language, Art, and Custom*, (New York: G. P. Putnam's Sons, 1920).

[83] Richard J. Gerrig, Roger R. Hook, and Philip G. Zimbardo, *An Overview of Psychology: Its Past and Present, Your Future*, custom ed, (Boston: allyn & Bacon, 2009); D. Brett King, Wayne Viney, and William Douglas Woody, *A History of Psychology: Ideas and Context*, 4th edition (Boston: Allyn & Bacon, 2009).

[84] Ibid.

[85] Ibid.

[86] Ibid.

[87] Ibid.

[88] Ibid.

[89] Ibid.

[90] Ibid.

[91] Ibid.

[92] Ibid.

[93] Ibid.

[94] Ibid.

[95] Ibid.

[96] Ibid.

[97] Ibid.

[98] Ibid.

[99] Ibid.

[100] Ibid

[101] W. S. C. Tisdall, "Comparative Religion," *The International Standard Bible Encyclopaedia,* 5 vols., ed. J. Orr, J. L. Nuelsen, E. Y. Mullins, & M. O. Evans (Chicago: The Howard-Severance Company, 1915), 692.

[102] Edward Burnett Tylor, *Primitive Culture: Research into the Development of Mythology, Philosophy, Religion, Language, Art, and Custom,* (New York: G. P. Putnam's Sons, 1920).

[103] Ibid

[104] Ibid

[105] Ibid

[106] Gerhard Kittel, Geoffrey W. Bromiley, and Gerhard Friedrich, eds., *Theological Dictionary of the New Testament* (Grand Rapids: Eerdmans, 1964)

[107] Ibid

[108] Edred Thorsson, *ALU: An Advanced Guide to Operative Runology.* (San Francisco: Weiser, 2012).

[109] R. Hogan, "The superstitions of everyday life". *Behavioral and Brain Sciences, 27*(6), 738-739. Retrieved from http://search.proquest.com/docview/212219404? accountid=34899

[110] Ibid.

[111] J. Mazur, (2005). *Learning and Behavior* [VitalSouce bookshelf version]. Retrieved from http://digitalbook shelf.argosy.edu/books/0558220231

[112] Ibid; R. Hogan, "The superstitions of everyday life". *Behavioral and Brain Sciences, 27*(6), 738-739. Retrieved from http://search.proquest.com/docview/212219404? accountid=34899.

[113] J. Mazur, (2005). *Learning and Behavior* [VitalSouce bookshelf version]. Retrieved from http://digitalbook shelf.argosy.edu/books/0558220231.

[114] Ibid.

[115] Ibid.

[116] Ibid.

[117] Ibid.

[118] FoxNews. (2012). 10 most sacred spots on Earth. Retrieved from http://www.foxnews.com/travel/2012/04/08/10-most-sacred-spots-on-earth/

[119] Ibid.

[120] Ibid.

[121] Ibid.

[122] Ibid.

[123] Ibid; R. Hogan, "The superstitions of everyday life". *Behavioral and Brain Sciences, 27*(6), 738-739. Retrieved from http://search.proquest.com/docview/212219404? accountid=34899

[124] J. Mazur, (2005). *Learning and Behavior* [VitalSouce bookshelf version]. Retrieved from http://digitalbook shelf.argosy.edu/books/0558220231

[125] Ibid.

[126] Ibid; FoxNews. (2012). 10 most sacred spots on Earth. Retrieved from http://www.foxnews.com/travel/2012/04/08/10-most-sacred-spots-on-earth/; R. Hogan, "The superstitions of everyday life". *Behavioral and Brain Sciences, 27*(6), 738-739. Retrieved from http://search.proquest.com/docview/212219404? accountid=34899

[127] Douglas T. Kenrick, Robert B. Cialdini, and Steven L. Nwwberg, *Social Psychology: Goals in Interaction*, 4th ed. (Boston: Allyn & Bacon, 2007).

[128] Ibid.

[129] Ibid.

[130] Ibid; John W. Santrock, *Life-Span Development*, 12th ed. (New York: McGraw-Hill Higher Education, 2009).

[131] Ibid.

[132] Ibid.

[133] Ibid.

[134] Ibid.

[135] Ibid.

[136] QuotesDaddy.com 2013. Retrieved from http://www.quotes daddy.com/author/John+Schumaker on April 5, 2013

[137] Joseph Campbell, *The Power of Myth with Bill Moyers* (New York: MJF Books, 1988), 103, 228.

[138] Feldman, R. S. *Child Development*, 6/e XML Vitalsource eBook for EDMC (6th ed). Pearson Learning Solutions. Retrieved from http://digitalbookshelf.argosy.edu/books/9781256507079/ id/ch09 box03.

[139] K. Hughes, (2011). Examiner.com. *Ritual, Psychology, Carl Jung and Archetypes*. Retrieved from http://www.examiner.com/ article/ritual-psychology-carl-jung-and-archetypes on April 8, 2013

[140] Stephen Flowers, Fire and Ice—*The History, Structure, and Rituals of Germany's Most Influential Modern Magical Order: The Brotherhood of Saturn* (St. Paul: Llewellyn Publications, 1994), 36.

[141] Feldman, R. S. *Child Development*, 6/e XML Vitalsource eBook for EDMC (6th ed). Pearson Learning Solutions. Retrieved from http://digitalbookshelf.argosy.edu/books/9781256507079/ id/ch09 box03.

[142] *Transcendental Magic, its Doctrine and Ritual*, trans. by A. E. Waite (London: George Redway, 1896), 3.

[143] Timothy W. Hogan, *Gnostic Reflections in Freemasonry*, "Freemason Information: A Web Magazine About Freemasonry." Published by Greg Stewart, July 9, 2009. Retrieved from http://freemasoninformation.com/2009/07/gnostic-reflections-in-freemasonry/

[144] W. P. Swainson, *Jacob Boehm: The Teutonic Philosopher* (London: William Rider & Son, LTD., 1921).

[145] *The Well Spring of the Goths: About the Gothic Peoples in the Nordic Countries and on the Continent* (New York: iUniverse, Inc., 2004), 72.

[146] Einherjar: Old Norse, single- or lone-fighters, also understood as "commanders-" or "warriors-of-one" (i.e., one's self). Another etymology of einherjar proposes that the word means "peerless warriors." There are a number of hero-sagas (e.g., Víkarr, Haralðr hílditann, Ívarr viðfamði, Haddingr, etc.) which are presumed to indicate individual initiations. Ibid, 68, 80; Galina Krasskova, *Exploring the Northern Tradition: A Guide to the Gods, Lore, Rites, and Celebrations from the Norse, German, and Anglo-Saxon Traditions* (Franklin Lakes: The Career Press, Inc., 2005), 133-134; John Lindow, *Handbook of Norse Mythology* (Santa Barbara: ABC-CLIO, Inc., 2001), 42, 58, 100, 104-105, 118.

[147] Snorri Sturluson, "Gylfaginning," *The Prose Edda*, trans. Arthur Gilchrist Brodeur (New York: The American Scandinavian Foundation, 1916).

[148] Bifrost: Old Norse, *Bifröst*, or, *Bilröst*, "the trembling path." Though the original form of the word is currently lost to antiquity, either rendition of the word suggests the idea and emphasizes the passing and delicate nature of both the rainbow and the bridge that the rainbow is here meant to typify as the path, portal, or bridge from Midgard, Middle-earth and home of humankind, to Asgard, home of the tribe of Norse Gods known as the Aesir. There is also

some conjecture that Bifrost may have originally been a reference to the Milky Way. Dan McCoy, *The Lore of Destiny: The Sacred and the Profane in Germanic Polytheism* (2013); *Norse Mythology for Smart People*, "Bifrost" (2016), retrieved from http://norse-mythology.org/cosmology/bifrost/; H. A. Guerber, *Myths of Northern Lands* (New York: American Book Co., 1895), 20-21, 26, 137; John Lindow, *Handbook of Norse Mythology*, (Santa Barbara: ABC-CLIO, Inc., 2001); 80-81; Kathleen N. Daly, *Norse Mythology A to Z* (New York: Chelsea House, 2010), 12; Viktor Rydberg, *Teutonic Mythology: Gods and Goddesses of the Northland* (New York: Norrœna Society, 1907), vol.1, 238; vol.2, 397-398, 466-468, 693-695, 814.

[149] Heimdall: Old Norse Heimdallr, one of the Aesir gods, is appointed with the task of being guardian of the gods' stronghold, Asgard, via his vigilant watch over the path/road from Asgard to Midgard, realm of humanity. Heimdall dwells in the "sky-cliffs" (lit. Himinbjörg) atop Bifrost and from there He watches and listens, ever at the ready to sound Gjallarhorn when intruders are approaching. At the onset of Ragnarok Heimdall will sound Gjallarhorn and signal the imminent arrival of those who would seek to storm Asgard and kill the gods. Kathleen N. Daly, *Norse Mythology A to Z* (New York: Chelsea House, 2010), xi, 39, 46-47, 82; H. A. Guerber, *Myths of Northern Lands*, (New York: American Book Co., 1895), 137; John Lindow, *Handbook of Norse Mythology*, (Santa Barbara: ABC-CLIO, Inc., 2001), 143-144; Ingemar Nordgren, *The Well Spring of the Goths: About the Gothic Peoples in the Nordic Countries and on the Continent.* (New York: iUniverse, Inc., 2004), 13, 18-19, 165-167.

[150] Vigrid, *the place on which battle surges*; Oskopnir, *the not created/not made*. Henry Adams Bellows, *The Poetic Edda*, The American Scandinavian Foundation (1923); Carolyne Larrington, *The Poetic*

Edda, Oxford University Press (1999); Andy Orchard, *Dictionary of Norse Myth and Legend*, Cassell (1997); Rudolf Simek, *Dictionary of Northern Mythology*, trans. by Angela Hall, D.S. Brewer (2007).

[151] James Allen Chisholm, "Grimnismal," *The Eddas: The Keys to the Mysteries of the North*, Internet Archive (open source), retrieved from https://archive.org/details/TheEddasTheKeysToTheMyst James AllenChisholmcf, stanzas 18, 36; "Vafthrudnismal," stanza 41.

[152] James Allen Chisholm, "Grimnismal," *The Eddas: The Keys to the Mysteries of the North*, Internet Archive (open source), retrieved from https://archive.org/details/TheEddasTheKeysToTheMyst James AllenChisholmcf, stanza 23.

[153] Ibid, stanzas 8-10.

[154] Ibid, stanza 61, note 21.

[155] *The Power of Myth* (New York: Anchor Books, 1991), 154.

[156] Theosophical University Press, 1985. Online edition retrieved from http://www.theosociety.org/pasadena/odin/odin-hp.htm.

[157] Ibid," 53-54.

[158] Kathleen N. Daly, *Norse Mythology A to Z* (New York: Chelsea House, 2010), 24.

[159] Germania of Tacitus, written c. 98 C.E.; Otto Hofler, *Kultische Geheimbunde der Germanen* (Frankfurt: M. Diesterweg, 1934); Bruce Lincoln, *Priests, Warriors, and Cattle: A Study in the Ecology of Religions* (Berkeley and Los Angeles: University of California Press, 1981), 122–133; John Lindow, *Handbook of Norse Mythology* (Santa Barbara: ABC-CLIO, Inc., 2001), 105; Ingemar Nordgren, *The Well Spring of the Goths: About the Gothic Peoples in the Nordic Countries and on the Continent* (New York: iUniverse, Inc., 2004), 68.

[160] Ingemar Nordgren, *The Well Spring of the Goths: About the Gothic Peoples in the Nordic Countries and on the Continent* (New York: iUniverse, Inc., 2004), 22, 63-66.

[161] Ibid, 8, 22, 61-63.

[162] Ibid, 22.

[163] Ibid.

[164] Ibid, 22, 26-27, 35, 55, 57, 65-66, 68, 71, 75.

[165] Dan McCoy, *The Lore of Destiny: The Sacred and the Profane in Germanic Polytheism* (2013); *Norse Mythology for Smart People*, "Bifrost" (2016), retrieved from http://norse-mythology.org/cosmology/bifrost/ ; H. A. Guerber, *Myths of Northern Lands* (New York: American Book Co., 1895), 20-21, 26, 137; John Lindow, *Handbook of Norse Mythology* (Santa Barbara: ABC-CLIO, Inc., 2001), 80-81; Kathleen N. Daly, *Norse Mythology A to Z* (New York: Chelsea House, 2010), 12; Viktor Rydberg, *Teutonic Mythology: Gods and Goddesses of the Northland* (New York: Norrœna Society, 1907), vol.1, 238; vol.2, 397-398, 466-468, 693-695, 814.

[166] Kathleen N. Daly, *Norse Mythology A to Z* (New York: Chelsea House, 2010), xi, 39, 46-47, 82; H. A. Guerber, *Myths of Northern Lands* (New York: American Book Co., 1895), 137; John Lindow, *Handbook of Norse Mythology* (Santa Barbara: ABC-CLIO, Inc., 2001), 143-144; Ingemar Nordgren, *The Well Spring of the Goths: About the Gothic Peoples in the Nordic Countries and on the Continent* (New York: iUniverse, Inc., 2004), 13, 18-19, 165-167.

[167] "Why the Opposition Doesn't Matter." ABN—Aesir Broadcasting Network, #24. Published Oct. 28, 2016. Retrieved from https://soundcloud.com/aesirbroadcasting/abn-bryan-wilton-why-the-opposition-doesnt-matter-24

[168] James Allen Chisholm, *The Eddas: The Keys to the Mysteries of the North*, Internet Archive (open source), retrieved from

https://archive.org/details/TheEddasTheKeysToTheMystJames AllenChisholm

[169] Kersey Graves, *The World's Sixteen Crucified Saviors*, retrieved from http://www.sacred-texts.com/bib/cv/wscs/index.htm

[170] Hávamál, stanzas 138 – 141

[171] Counter-Currents Publishing, 4/29/2011. Retrieved from http://www.counter-currents.com/2011/04/what-god-did-odin-worship/

[172] Bryan Wilton, ABN: Aesir Broadcasting Network, "Tacitus on the Germans," published January 18, 2017. Retrieved from https://soundcloud.com/aesirbroadcasting/abn-bryan-wilton-tacitus-on-the-germans-53

[173] Samael Aun Weor, *Introduction to Gnosis: Gnostic Methods for Today's World* (Glorian Publishing, 2009); Stephan A. Hoeller, *Gnosticism: New Light on the Ancient Tradition of Inner Knowing* (Wheaton, Il.: Quest Books, 2002).

[174] (New York, NY: Norrœna Society, 1907), vol. 2, 406.

[175] Kenith Sylvan Guthrie, trans., and David Fideler, ed. The Pythagorean Sourcebook and Library (Grand Rapids, MI.: Phanes Press, 1988), 133.

[176] ABN—Aesir Broadcasting Network "Why the Opposition Doesn't Matter." Published Oct. 28, 2016. Retrieved from https://soundcloud.com/aesirbroadcasting/abn-bryan-wilton-why-the-opposition-doesnt-matter-24

[177] At just twenty years old Benjamin Franklin recorded his methodical approach toward becoming a virtuous man. Benjamin Franklin listed out thirteen virtues for which he wished to demonstrate each day with increasing frequency. The system he used not only aided in his daily demonstration of the virtues, but it allowed him a method by which he could monitor his progress as well. Benjamin Franklin came up with his own list of eleven virtues

which he wanted to implement more in his life. Those eleven virtues, to Bro. Franklin encapsulated his idea of the virtuous man.

[178] The Nine Noble Virtues were originally constructed by the Committee for the Restoration of the Odinic Rite back in the early 1970s (Stephen McNallen, *Asatru: A Native European Spirituality* (Nevada City, CA: Runestone Press, 2015), 89-90). The Nine Noble Virtues are a list which Odinist/Asatru Folk have found encapsulates those noble characteristics expressed most often by our gods and heroes within our myths, poems, and folk lore.

[179] Edred Thorsson, *ALU: An Advanced Guide to Operative Runology*, (San Francisco, CA: Weiser Books, 2012), 166.

[180] *The Power of Myth with Bill Moyers* (New York: MJF Books, 1988), 206.

BIBLIOGRAPHY

American Association of Pastoral Counselors (2012). *Code of Ethics*. Retrieved from http://aapc.org/Default.aspx?ssid= 74&NavPTypeId=1161

American Counseling Association (2005). *Code of Ethics and Standards of Practice*. Retrieved from http://www.counseling.org/ Resources/aca-code-of-ethics.pdf

American Psychological Association. (2010). *American Psychological Association: Ethical Principles of Psychologists and Code of Conduct*. Retrieved from http://www.apa.org/ethics/code/ principles.pdf

Antonsen, Elmer H. "On the Mythological Interpretation of the Oldest Runic Inscriptions," in *Languages and Cultures: Studies in Honor of Edgar C. Polome*. Mohammard ali Jazayy and Werner Winter, eds. New York: Mouton de Gruyter, 1988.

Arvidsson, Stefan. *Aryan Idols: Indo-European Mythology as Ideology and Science*, trans. Sonia Wichmann. Chicago: University of Chicago Press, 2006.

Barnes, L. P. and Kay, W. K. "Developments in Religious Education in England and Wales (Part 2): Methodology, Politics, Citizenship and School Performance," *Themelios* 25, no. 3. 2000.

Barry, Kieren. *The Greek Qabalah: Alphabetic Mysticism and Numerology in the Ancient World*. York Beach: Samuel Weiser, Inc., 1999.

Barton, John. *The Cambridge Companion to Biblical Interpretation*. New York: Cambridge University Press, 1998.

Bedard, Moe. *The Order of the Gnostics: Ancient Teachings for the Modern Gnostic*. Moeseo, Inc., 2015.

Bellows, Henry Adams. *The Poetic Edda.* The American Scandinavian Foundation, 1923.

Besant, Annie. *Esoteric Christianity.* London: The Theosophical Publishing Society, 1905.

Branagh, Kenneth. *Thor.* Hollywood: Paramount Pictures, 2011.

Brand, Chad, et al., eds., "Hermetic Literature," *Holman Illustrated Bible Dictionary.* Nashville, TN: Holman Bible Publishers, 2003.

Callahan, Tim. *Secret Origins of the Bible.* Altadena: Millennium Press, 2002.

Campbell, Joseph. *The Power of Myth with Bill Moyers.* New York: MJF Books, 1988.

Carlile, Richard. *Manuel of Freemasonry.* Leeds: Celephais Press, 2005.

Case, Paul Foster. *Esoteric Secrets of Meditation & Magic.* Fraternity of the Hidden Light, 2008.

Chisholm, James Allen. *The Eddas: The Keys to the Mysteries of the North.* Internet Archive (open source). Retrieved from https://archive.org/details/TheEddasTheKeysToTheMyst James AllenChisholm.

Cleary, Collin. *What God Did Odin Worship.* Counter-Currents Publishing, 4/29/2011. Retrieved from http://www.counter-currents.com/2011/04/what-god-did-odin-worship/

Cooke, Bernard and Macy, Gary. *Christian Symbol and Ritual: An Introduction.* New York: Oxford University Press, 2005.

Davidson, H. R. Ellis. *Gods & Myths of Northern Europe.* London: Penguin Books Ltd, 1990.

Daly, Kathleen N. *Norse Mythology A to Z*. New York: Chelsea House, 2010.

De Benoise, Alain. *On Being a Pagan*, trans. Joh Graham, ed. Greg Johnson, pref. Stephen Edred Flowers. Atlanta: ULTRA, 2004.

DeMaris, Richard E. *The New Testament in its Ritual World*. New York: Routledge, 2008.

Ephron, Nora. Michael. Turner Pictures/New Line Cinema, 1996.

Evans, C. S. *Pocket Dictionary of Apologetics & Philosophy of Religion*. Downers Grove: InterVarsity Press, 2002.

Fee, Gordon and Stuart, Douglas. *How to Read the Bible for all its Worth*. Grand Rapids: Zondervan, 2003.

Feldman, R. S. *Child Development*, 6/e XML Vitalsource eBook for EDMC (6th ed). Pearson Learning Solutions. Retrieved from http://digitalbookshelf.argosy.edu/books/9781256507079/id/ch09 box03

Flowers, Stephen E. *Fire and Ice—The History, Structure, and Rituals of Germany's Most Influential Modern Magical Order: The Brotherhood of Saturn*. St. Paul: Llewellyn Publications, 1994.

———— *Lords of the Left Hand Path: A History of Spiritual Dissent*. Smithville: Rune-Raven Press, 1997.

———— *Restoring the Indo-European Religion*. Red Ice TV, published March 16, 2016. Retrieved from https://www.youtube.com/watch?v=VomiUEsqvAg

———— "Toward an Archaic Germanic Psychology," in *Journal of Indo-European Studies*. Austin, University of Texas, n.d.

Foutz, Scott David "Universal Mysticism and the Christian Theistic Paradigm," *Quodlibet Journal* 1, no. 7, November 1999, http://www.quodlibet.net/articles/foutz-mystic.shtml.

FoxNews. (2012). 10 Most Sacred Spots on Earth. Retrieved from http://www.foxnews.com/travel/ 2012/04/08/10-most-sacred-spots-on-earth/

Frawley, David. *Wisdom of the Ancient Seers: Mantras of the Rig Veda.* Salt Lake City: Passage Press, 1992.

Gerrig, Richard J. *An Overview of Psychology: Its Past and Present, Your Future*, Custom Ed. Boston: Allyn & Bacon, 2009.

Gerrig, Richard J. and Zimbardo, Philip G. *Psychology and Life, Discovering Psychology Edition.* Boston: Allyn & Bacon, 2009.

Graves, Kersey. *The World's Sixteen Crucified Saviors*, retrieved from http://www.sacred-texts.com/bib/cv/wscs/index.htm

Guerber, H. A. *Myths of Northern Lands.* New York: American Book Co., 1895.

Gunnarsson, Sturla. Beowulf & Grendel. Truly Indie, 2005.

Gunther, Hans F. K. *The Religious Attitude of the Indo-Europeans*, Vivian Bird, trans. London: Clair Press, 1963.

Guthrie, Kenith Sylvan. *The Pythagorean Sourcebook and Library.* Grand Rapids, MI.: Phanes Press, 1988.

Hall, Manly P. *The Wisdom of the Knowing Ones.* Los Angeles: Philosophical Research Society, 2000.

Heindel, Max. *Parsifal: Wagner's Famous Mystic Music Drama.* "Rosicrucian Christianity", Series no. 12. Oceanside: The Rosicrucian Fellowship, 1909.

Hoeller, Stephan A. *Gnosticism: New Light on the Ancient Tradition of Inner Knowing.* Wheaton: Quest Books, 2002.

———— *The Gnostic Jung and the Seven Sermons to the Dead.* Wheaton: Quest Books, 1982.

Hofler, Otto. *Kultische Geheimbunde der Germanen.* Frankfurt: M. Diesterweg, 1934.

Hogan, R. "The Superstitions of Everyday Life". *Behavioral and Brain Sciences,* 27(6). Retrieved from http://search. proquest.com/docview/212219404? accountid=34899

Hogan, Timothy W. "Gnostic Reflections in Freemasonry," *Freemason Information: A Web Magazine About Freemasonry.* Published by Greg Stewart, July 9, 2009. Retrieved from http://freemasoninformation.com/2009/07/gnostic-reflections-in-freemasonry/

Hood, Ralph W., Jr. "Psychology of Religion," encyclopedia of Religion and Society, William H. Swatos (ed.). Retrieved from http://www.hirr.hartsem.edu/ency/Psychology.htm

Hughes, K. (2011). Examiner.com. *Ritual, Psychology, Carl Jung and Archetypes.* Retrieved from http://www.examiner.com/article/ritual-psychology-carl-jung-and-archetypes on April 8, 2013

Hulse, David Allen. *New Dimensions for the Cube of Space: The Path of Initiation Revealed by the Tarot upon the Qabalistic Cube.* York Beach: Samuel Weiser, Inc., 2000.

Inman, Thomas. *Ancient Pagan and Modern Christian Symbolism.* New York: J. W. Bouton, 1884.

Janawitz, Naomi. *Magic in the Roman World: Pagans, Jews, and Christians.* New York: Routledge, 2001.

Jung, Carl. *Essay on Wotan* [First published as WOTAN, Neue Schweizer Rundschau (Zurich). n.s., III (March, 1936), 657-69. Republished in Aufsatze Zurzeitgeschichte (Zurich, 1946), 1-23. Trans. by Barbara Hannah in Essays on Contemporary Events (London, 1947), 1-16; this version has been consulted. Motto, trans. by H.C. Roberts:] Retrieved from http://www.philosopher.eu/others-writings/essay-on-wotan-w-nietzsche-c-g-jung/

———— *Psychology and Religion*. New York: Routledge, 2008.

Kenrick, Douglas. *Social Psychology: Goals in Interaction*, 4th ed. Boston: Allyn & Bacon, 2007.

King, D. Brett, *A History of Psychology: Ideas and Context*, 4th edition. Boston: Allyn & Bacon, 2009.

Kittel, Gerhard. (ed.) *Theological Dictionary of the New Testament*. Grand Rapids: Eerdmans, 1964.

Krasskova, Galina. *Exploring the Northern Tradition: A Guide to the Gods, Lore, Rites, and Celebrations from the Norse, German, and Anglo-Saxon Traditions*. Franklin Lakes: The Career Press, Inc., 2005.

Larrington, Carolyne. *The Poetic Edda*. Oxford University Press, 1999.

Levi, Eliphas. *Transcendental Magic, its Doctrine and Ritual*, trans. by A. E. Waite. London: George Redway, 1896.

Lincoln, Bruce. *Priests, Warriors, and Cattle: A Study in the Ecology of Religions*. Berkeley and Los Angeles: University of California Press, 1981.

Lindow, John. *Handbook of Norse Mythology*. Santa Barbara: ABC-CLIO, Inc., 2001.

Linzie, Bil, *Drinking at the Well of Mimir: An Asatru Man's Meanderings Through the Last 30 Years.* Dec. 2000. Retrieved from http://www.heathengods.com/library/bil_linzie/well_of_mimir.pdf.

———— *Germanic Spirituality.* July 2003. Retrieved from http://www.heathengods.com/library/bil_linzie/germanic_spirituality.pdf.

———— *Investigating the Afterlife Concepts of the Norse Heathen: A Reconstructionist's Approach.* Dec. 2005. Retrieved from http://www.heathengods.com/library/bil_linzie/after_life_bil_linzie.pdf.

———— *Uncovering the Effects of Cultural Background on the Reconstruction of Ancient Worldviews.* March 2004. Retrieved from http://www.heathengods.com/library/bil_linzie/cultural_background.pdf.

Lucas, George. *Star Wars,* 1977. Lucasfilm Ltd., 20th Century Fox Home Entertainment, 2011, Blu-ray Disc.

Mackenzie, Donald A. *Teutonic Myth and Legend: An Introduction to the Eddas & Sagas, Beowolf, The Nibelungenlied, etc.* London: Gresham Publications, 1912.

Matasouie, Ranko. *A Reader in Comparative Indo-European Religion.* Zageb: University of Zageb, 2010.

Mazur, J. (2005). Learning and Behavior [VitalSouce bookshelf version]. Retrieved from http://digitalbookshelf.argosy.edu/books/0558220231

McCoy, Dan. *The Lore of Destiny: The Sacred and the Profane in Germanic Polytheism* (2013); *Norse Mythology for Smart People* (2016). Retrieved from http://norse-mythology.org.

McNallen, Stephen A. *Ancestral Roots & Metagenetics*. Red Ice TV, published July 12, 2014. Retrieved from https://www.youtube.com/watch?v=B546mQQZ-sE&t=270s

——— *Asatru: A Native European Spirituality*. Nevada City: Runestone Press, 2015.

——— "Three decades of the Asatru Revival in America," in *Tyr: Myth—Culture—Tradition, Volume 2*, ed. Joshua Buckley and Michael Moynihan (Atlanta: Ultra Publishing, 2004/2008), 219.

McVan, Ron. *The Temple of Wotan: Holy Book of the Aryan Tribes*. St. Maries: Fourteen Word Press, 2000.

——— *Creed of Iron: Wotansvolk Wisdom* and *Temple of Wotan: Holy Book of the Aryan Tribes*. St. Maries: Fourteen Word Press, 1997.

Mead, G. R. S. trans. *Pistis Sophia*. The Gnostic Society Library, Gnostic Scriptures and Fragments. Retrieved from http://www.gnosis.org/library/pistis-sophia/index.htm

Meyer, J. and Land, R. *Threshold Concepts and Troublesome Knowledge: Linkages to Ways of Thinking and Practicing Within the Disciplines*, 2003. Retrieved from: www.etl.tla.ed.ac.uk/docs/ETLreport4.pdf

Morris, Charles. *Aryan Sun-Myths: The Origin of Religions*. New York: Nims and Knight, 1889.

Nordgren, Ingemar. *The Well Spring of the Goths: About the Gothic Peoples in the Nordic Countries and on the Continent*. New York: iUniverse, Inc., 2004.

Orchard, Andy. *Dictionary of Norse Myth and Legend*. Cassell, 1997.

Patheos Online Religious Library: *South America.* http://www.patheos.com/Library/South-American

PBS. *From Jesus to Christ.* Frontline series, 4 parts, April, 1998. Full program with student and teacher's guide retrieved from http://www.pbs.org/wgbh/pages/frontline/shows/religio n/watch/

Pike, Albert. *Indo-Aryan Deities and Worship—As Contained in the Rig Veda.* Louisville: Standard Printing Co., 1930.

———— *Morals and Dogma of the Ancient and Accepted Scottish Rite of Freemasonry.* Charleston, 1871. Retrieved from https://archive.org/details/moralsdogmaofanc00pikeiala.

QuotesDaddy.com 2013. Retrieved from http://www.quotes daddy.com/author/John+Schumaker on April 5, 2013

Rayner, Dan. *Asatru Mindset & Reinvigorating the European Spirit.* Red Ice TV, published July 21, 2014. Retrieved from https://www.youtube.com/watch?v=j3KEbgdCBBA&t= 2217s

Rees, T. "God," *The International Standard Bible Encyclopaedia,* 5 vols., ed. J. Orr, J. L. Nuelsen, E. Y. Mullins, & M. O. Evans. Chicago: The Howard-Severance Company, 1915.

Robinson, B. A. "World Religions—Asatru: Norse Heathenism," *Ontario Consultants on Religious Tolerance,* 1997-2011. http://www.religioustolerance.org/asatru.htm.

Rubarth, Scott. "Stoic Philosophy of Mind." *Internet Encyclopedia of Philosophy: A Peer-Reviewed Academic Resource.* Retrieved from www.iep.utm.edu/stoicmind/

Russell, James C. *The Germanization of Early Medieval Christianity: A Sociohistorical Approach to Religious Transformation.* New York: Oxford University Press, 1994.

Rydberg, Viktor. *Teutonic Mythology: Gods and Goddesses of the Northland.* Vol. 1-3. New York: Norrœna Society, 1907.

Santrock, John W. *Life-Span Development,* 12th ed. New York: McGraw-Hill Higher Education, 2009.

Semetsky, Inna. *The Edusemiotics of Images: Essays on the Art-Science of Tarot.* Boston: Sense Publishers, 2013.

Simek, Rudolf. *Dictionary of Northern Mythology,* trans. by Angela Hall. D.S. Brewer, 2007.

Simon. *Papal Magic: Occult Practices Within the Catholic Church.* New York: HarperCollins Publishers, Inc., 2007.

Smoley, Richard. *Inner Christianity: A Guide to the Esoteric Tradition.* Boston: Shambhala Publications, Inc., 2002.

Steiner, Rudolf. *An Outline of Esoteric Science,* trans. Catherine E. Creeger. Hudson: Anthroposophic Press, 1997.

———— *Angels, Archangels of the Folk and Myths of Northern Europe.* Lecture 1, 1919; published 2015. Retrieved from https://www.youtube.com/watch?v=frw0uuMKl-I

Sturluson, Snorri. "Gylfaginning," *The Prose Edda,* trans. Arthur Gilchrist Brodeur. New York: The American Scandinavian Foundation, 1916.

Swainson, W. P. *Jacob Boehm: The Teutonic Philosopher.* London: William Rider & Son, LTD., 1921.

Taliaferro, Charles. "Philosophy of Religion", *The Stanford Encyclopedia of Philosophy* (Winter 2014 Edition), Edward N. Zalta (ed.). Retrieved from https://plato.stanford.edu/entries/philosophy-religion/

The Wachawski Brothers. *The Matrix,* 1999. Warner Bros., Warner Home Entertainment, 2009, Blu-ray Disc.

Thorsson, Edred. *A Book of Troth*. Smithsville: Runa-Raven Press, 2003.

———— *ALU: An Advanced Guide to Operative Runology*. San Francisco: Weiser, 2012.

———— *Northern Magic: Rune Mysteries and Shamanism*. Woodbury: Llewellyn Publications, 2005.

———— *Runelore: A Handbook of Esoteric Runology*. York Beach: Weiser, 1987.

Tisdall, W. S. C. "Comparative Religion," *The International Standard Bible Encyclopaedia*, 5 vols., ed. J. Orr, J. L. Nuelsen, E. Y. Mullins, & M. O. Evans. Chicago: The Howard-Severance Company, 1915.

Titchenell, Elsa-Brita. *The Masks of Odin: Wisdom of the Ancient Norse*. Theosophical University Press, 1985. Online edition retrieved from http://www.theosociety.org/pasadena/odin/odin-hp.htm.

Tylor, Edward Burnett. *Primitive Culture: Research into the Development of Mythology, Philosophy, Religion, Language, Art, and Custom*. New York: G. P. Putnam's Sons, 1920.

Tyson, Donald. New Millennium Magic: A Complete System of Self-Realization. St. Paul: Llewellyn Publications, 1996.

Waite, Arthur Edward. *The Way of Divine Union*. London: William Rider & Son, Ltd., 1915.

Weimer, Maryellen. "Threshold Concepts: Portals to New Ways of Thinking," in *Faculty Focus: Higher Ed Teaching Strategies from Magna Publications*, November 7, 2014. Retrieved from www.facultyfocus.com/articles/teaching-and-learning/threshold-concepts-portals-new-ways-thinking/

Weor, Samael Aun. *Introduction to Gnosis: Gnostic Methods for Today's World*. Glorian Publishing, 2009.

West, Shelly. *Kabbalistic Psychology*. Gnostic Warrior, published February 1, 2017. Retrieved from gnosticwarrior.com/shelly-west-2.html.

Wilton, Bryan. "Tacitus on the Germans," ABN—Aesir Broadcasting Network. Published January 18, 2017. Retrieved from https://soundcloud.com/aesirbroadcasting/abn-bryan-wilton-tacitus-on-the-germans-53

——— "Why the Opposition Doesn't Matter." ABN—Aesir Broadcasting Network. Published Oct. 28, 2016. Retrieved from https://soundcloud.com/aesirbroadcasting/abn-bryan-wilton-why-the-opposition-doesnt-matter-24.

ABOUT THE AUTHOR

Roland is one of the leading educators in the field of Esoteric Traditions, Gnostic Philosophy, and the Odinic Mysteries for today's Norse spiritual warriors. With his blog, *The Way of the Einherjar: Gnostic Warriors of the North*; his online study platform, *Runekenhof: Temple of the Northern Mystery Tradition*; his local Asatru kindred, *Folkgard of Holda & Odin*; and, his desk-top publishing business, *Har's Hall*, Roland is dedicated to empowering indigenous Europeans with the *gnosis* essential for their collective and individual spiritual healing and conscious "re"-awakening. Roland has earned seminary degrees in Metaphysics (DM) and Comparative Religion (MA), and an academic degree in Psychology (BA). He is an Alpha Theta Delta inductee in the Phi Theta Kappa international collegiate honor society. In the past, Roland has also written ecclesiastical curriculum for instruction in Esoteric Christianity, Metaphysics, and Spiritual Alchemy and Pathworking. Most recently, Roland has begun collaboration with others to establish and operate a radio show and podcast focusing on the gnostic element of the Northern Wisdom Tradition.

Made in the USA
Monee, IL
24 November 2020

49493099R00164